ENDORSEMENTS

This book is excellent!

From the moment I started reading Annette's book, it became very clear that this was the work of a tenured prophetic voice. She speaks as one having authority earned through a lifetime of encounters with the Holy Spirit. She masterfully covers issues in prophecy that very few would dare address.

Halfway through reading her book, I began experiencing what Psalm 42:7 refers to as "the deep calling to deep." Annette's words induced prophetic revelation to come alive, and this will likely be the experience of many who read this book. You will discover her insight and wisdom regarding prophecy is informative, revelatory, and empowering.

A tremendous point of interest are a number of very relevant and powerful prophecies given by Annette's father, whom many would consider a general in the faith, Charles Capps.

I highly recommend this book to every believer. You will come away with a heightened understanding of the spirit of prophecy. It is a must have!

—**Joseph Z**
Founder of Zministries
Host of Prophecy LIVE
JosephZ.Com

My friend, Annette Capps, has written a most important book! As you read with an open mind, you will learn how the human consciousness interacts with the Spirit of the living God. If there's ever been a time when it is imperative that we understand the spirit of prophecy, it is now! How can we judge prophecy if we do not have a biblical view of the gifts God has provided for us—to bring us into a position where the spirit world is our reality? If you desire a better understanding of the relationship, the flow of divine energy between the spirit, soul, and body in a world of polarity, this book is for you.

For me, this book is an answer to prayer. As a Bible teacher, I desperately wanted to know how to answer those who teach that prophecy and other gifts of the Spirit passed away with the apostles. I know believers who love God's Word but have chosen to believe that we no longer need these spiritual tools operating in our churches today. Yet, we need everything that God has provided for us

As you read about Annette Capps's personal experiences that began in her childhood and the scriptural truths she has searched out, your interest and motivation to know God will increase. Just as I did, you will delight in her spiritual adventures; sometimes laughing—other times brought to tears. Take time to experience this taste of fresh water flowing from the throne of God through the pen of a ready writer. Many have benefited, grown spiritually, and received healing from her obedience.

My friend and I have followed a similar trajectory throughout our spiritual journeys. I'll always cherish the time God gave her insight into a situation that caused me great anxiety. After listening to me, she spoke a prophecy in conversational tone that changed my life. There was no drama, and it was later that I recognized her words were from the heart of the Father.

The Spirit of Prophecy will delight you and challenge you to know God more intimately. For the spiritual seeker there are clear steppingstones that lead you through a portal into that secret place where you will experience the presence and power of God. I consider *The Spirit of Prophecy* an essential book for all who yearn to walk in anointed paths of righteousness. You are here for such a time as this to proclaim the wonders of our victorious Lord to all who will hear, and future generations will arise and glorify the King of Kings and Lord of Lords!

The prophecies in this book given by her dad, Brother Charles Capps, will encourage you, and together, we shall see all God-given prophecies come to pass to the glory of our Father God.

—**Germaine Copeland**
Author of the Prayers That Avail Much® book series
President of Prayers That Avail Much Ministries (aka Word
Ministries, Inc.)
Monroe, Georgia

You can prophesy! This book is a road map for every Christian who desires to see a revival of the prophetic Word of God in his or her life and in the body of Christ. Between these pages, you'll develop a deeper relationship with the Spirit of Prophecy and learn how He operates in the Church. I really believe that this book is a bridge between two worlds in the body of Christ that desperately need to coexist in the last days. This book will become required reading for our leadership, and, in fact, it is a must read for every end-time believer!

—Alan Didio

Annette Capps, a master teacher and author, commonly takes what can seem like complex scriptures and offer a sound and solid interpretation. She skillfully breaks down scriptures, so not only do you understand them, but you are inspired and enabled to act on the truth in them.

In *The Spirit of Prophecy*, Annette writes as an experienced interpreter and guide for those who want clarity of the scope and function of the spirit of prophecy in the realm of the spirit.

This book serves as an excellent handbook and guide for those who desire to learn to walk and work with God in the vast frontier lands of the spirit yet to be discovered.

—Patsy Cameneti
Co-Pastor Rhema Family Church
Brisbane, Australia

the SPIRIT *of* PROPHECY

Harrison House

Shippensburg, PA

A PORTAL TO THE
PRESENCE AND POWER OF GOD

the SPIRIT of
PROPHECY

ANNETTE CAPPS

Published by Harrison House Publishers
Shippensburg, PA 17257

ISBN 13 TP: 978-1-6803-1889-0

ISBN 13 eBook: 978-1-6803-1890-6

ISBN 13 Hardcover: 978-1-6675-0037-9

For Worldwide Distribution.

1 2 3 4 5 6 7 8 / 26 25 24 23 22

CONTENTS

"Worship God! For the testimony of Jesus is the spirit of prophecy."

Revelation 19:10

PREFACE

For those who are familiar with my other books and writings, this may seem like a departure from my *usual* style of writing…and you are correct. This book is not meant to be a teaching book with an expansion of ideas developed upon a careful, analytical study of Bible passages from the Greek and Hebrew. (Which I love, by the way.)

I want to share what the Holy Spirit has taught me about the things of the Spirit and what I have learned from seasoned ministers. These men and women have roots in the Pentecostal Movement of the early 1900s, the healing and tent revivals of the '40s and '50s, and the Charismatic Movement of the '70s and '80s.

Names like Aimee Semple McPherson, William Branham, Oral Roberts, Jack Coe, Kenneth E. Hagin, Vicki Jamison Peterson, and of course—Charles Capps. These are my roots. My early guidance about the workings of the Spirit came from my Grandmother Capps who was often given information and direct guidance through visions and dreams. From her, I heard stories about the tent meetings she attended with many of the names mentioned above.

I could give you a detailed outline of study about the gifts of the Spirit. But many excellent books have been written by authors such as Kenneth E. Hagin and Donald Gee. This book is not an in-depth study of "the gift of prophecy" but a presentation of the "spirit of prophecy" and how it flows.

As I was in the process of writing, I "coincidentally" found a file in storage that contained transcriptions of prophetic words given through my dad 30 to 40 years ago. They have been kept hidden until now. I am sharing some of them in this book, but I fully intend to publish most of them in a separate book in the near future.

This entire book is for you to prayerfully consider and hopefully receive the anointing from those who have gone before us. It's time to press forward, shake aside *our* traditions, and move into the next great move of the Holy Spirit. *It's time for the latter rain.*

—**Annette Capps**
October 19, 2021

THE ENCOUNTER

As the double doors of the church entryway opened, congregation members were met with a mess or a miracle, depending on their point of view. Disheveled, crying, and shouting preteens and teenagers were all over the sanctuary. One was dancing the dance of the Spirit between the pews with eyes closed, and many were speaking in tongues.

A girl my age was in the middle of the sanctuary on the left side—near the pew where my great grandmother always sat. She was lying prostrate on the floor with eyes closed, spinning like a top. Under the control of the Spirit, she navigated up and down the rows of pews, spinning parallel to the floor.

I cannot explain how she did that and finally quit trying. You could never say she was spinning in her own ability. From what I saw, it was physically impossible for her to do what she did.

Parents and church members gathered in the pews at the back of the church. They sat wide-eyed and speechless. Parents had received phone calls at midnight from their sobbing children, and they desperately tried to find out what happened.

The only thing they could gather was that Jesus was at the church. I am not certain, but I think they were frightened.

With each adult who entered the sanctuary, the Presence of God decreased in intensity. It was as if part of the Spirit left every time the back door opened.

What do you do with a bunch of young people who say they saw Jesus and seemed to be having an experience with God, but you have never seen or experienced anything like that?

Who knows how to conclude a meeting where the Holy Spirit took over? Do you stand up and say, "Now let's dismiss in prayer?" That would feel sacrilegious. How do you dismiss the Spirit of God or exit His Presence? Do you ask Him to *let go of you*? Or let you *go home*?

The details are fuzzy. But we all managed to leave and somehow got home. I don't think one adult understood what happened to us. But it changed us forever.

The year was 1968, and I was 14 years old when I experienced this mighty move of God. My recollection of these events is as vivid today as it was then. It was an outpouring of the Spirit, similar to the Day of Pentecost in the book of Acts.

> *When the day of Pentecost came, they were all together in one place. Suddenly a sound like the blowing of a violent wind came from heaven and filled the whole house where they were sitting. They saw what seemed to be tongues of fire that separated and came to rest on each of them. All of*

them were filled with the Holy Spirit and began to speak in other tongues as the Spirit enabled them.

Acts 2:1-4 NIV

These verses from the book of Acts show how the prophecy of Joel 2:28-29 was fulfilled among an unlikely group of people in the city of Jerusalem. They were men and women from every walk of life and did not have what was considered a "proper" education in the scriptures. They were not part of an "elite" group. Nor did they hold powerful positions in the synagogue. Instead, they were fishermen, tax collectors, prostitutes, and laborers. These common people believed the testimony of Jesus. And it was upon them that the Spirit manifested in flames of fire and speaking in tongues.

And it was upon another unlikely gathering of young people in England, Arkansas that God's power fell in the summer of 1968 in a supernatural display of the Holy Spirit.

CHAPTER 1

HUNGRY FOR A MOVE OF GOD

Although I was raised in a Pentecostal denomination, my church never had much of a display of the gifts of the Spirit. Occasionally, we had tongues and interpretation when the Spirit was "really moving." However, I was aware that supernatural manifestations of the Holy Spirit were possible.

I had seen God's Presence sweep into the church youth camp services I attended each summer in Hot Springs, Arkansas. The Holy Spirit had free course there. I witnessed repentance, salvation, and rejoicing among those hungry youth. Each night the altars were filled with seekers. Young people seeking the baptism of the Holy Spirit with the evidence of speaking in tongues and seeking God. Seeking to know Him. Seeking His Presence. Seeking His touch.

Some youth had visions of Jesus, and their lives were forever transformed. Others received the infilling of the Holy Spirit. They spoke in tongues into the early morning hours with a heavenly glow radiating from their faces. At times, the bodies of young people covered the floor at the front of the auditorium with the power of God holding them in His glory.

That same revival spirit never manifested in our local churches. I confirmed this with other youth at camp the following year. They experienced the same "letdown" that I did. When we returned to our churches, we shared our life-changing experiences. Although church members rejoiced at the reports, they patted us on the back and said, "Now, let's get back to 'regular' church." And the mighty move of God that started in camp was quenched in us.

What we had experienced at camp was real, and we wanted to live our lives in the Presence of God and please Him. I wasn't sure what we could have done to keep that fire burning in our youth group.

(My perspective as an adult is somewhat different. It is perplexing for adults to be confronted with outstanding spiritual experiences from the younger generation when they have no personal context. Encouragement, however, was better than being discouraged!)

The next time I returned home "on fire for God"—fresh from the power and anointing of the Holy Spirit—I called a council of young people.

The youth group in our church was small but close. As one of the few Pentecostal churches in a small town, we endured the mocking attitude of being persecuted because we were "tongue talkers." What the townspeople didn't know was that there wasn't much "tongue talking" and "wildfire" going on.

After getting permission from the pastor, the youth group met at the church on a Friday night. Our goal was to pray for revival and for people to be saved.

We gathered around the old wooden bench altars at the front of the church. Those altars had seen three generations of my family saved and filled with the Holy Spirit. They had spent many hours praying and seeking God around them.

God had moved upon my great grandparents and grandparents to help get our church started. They even worked on the construction of the building.

A Rich Spiritual History

My ancestors were farmers, not preachers. They were part of the Pentecostal outpouring (and persecution) in north Arkansas around 1905. Seeking to find better farmland for their crops, they loaded their cow, pig, chickens, and household belongings on a train to purchase their share of the rich Delta farmland between the Arkansas and Mississippi rivers. When they discovered there was no Pentecostal church where they could worship God in the power of the Spirit with signs and wonders, they decided to start one.

As a 14-year-old who had encountered a supernatural God at camp, I wanted to know what happened to the signs and wonders? Why did they stop? I was determined to find out at those same altars that had seen the glory of God. Something had been lost.

My grandmother told me how I was healed of pneumonia at six months of age. The healing evangelist, Jack Coe, held a prayer cloth in his hands and prayed for God's healing power to go into that cloth. He prayed according to Acts 19:12 where handkerchiefs and aprons that had touched Paul were taken to the sick, and the diseases and evil spirits left the people. When my grandmother laid the prayer cloth on my sick body, I was healed.

My grandparents had often traveled to the great tent meetings of Jack Coe, Oral Roberts, William Branham, and A.A. Allen. Some of the tales they told about these meetings seemed to be embedded in my DNA. Healings, miracles, and supernatural deliverances were part of my physical and spiritual heritage. But where did this wonderful wealth of history go? Had it been forgotten?

Our "Upper Room" Experience

Your young men [youth] *will see visions.*

Acts 2:17 NLT

Arkansas summers are hot and humid. That night, the temperature was just cooling down when the youth group arrived at the church.

We began praying in the early evening hours. As the youth prayed around the altar benches, it appeared to be an ordinary prayer meeting. Quiet murmuring on bended knees, with heads bowed and elbows resting on the slick wooden altar benches stained with tears. We began by praying for people we knew who needed to be saved.

From our hearts came intercession for family members, friends from school, and people who came to our minds. The amount of time we prayed is not in my memory now, having been jolted by what happened next. It was not the gentle descent of a dove that came upon us but a sudden blast of power exploding in the church auditorium. I was flattened by it and knocked on my back.

As the heavenly language of tongues rolled from my lips, I was vaguely aware of loud crying, repenting, and praising God. Sounds of young people speaking in tongues filled the room. I was in the holy Presence of God, and nothing happening around me mattered.

Around 10 o'clock, with everyone still around the altars, the spirit of prophecy came upon me. Until that moment, I couldn't get off the floor. When I got up, it felt like an unseen force moved me to the pulpit on the elevated stage. To my utter amazement, I preached and prophesied under the anointing of the Holy Spirit for almost an hour.

Some of the youth were still crying when I exhorted them to repent and be saved. Little did I know that several of our church-attending young people had never been born again.

Church attendance and lip service to faith do not equal salvation. A personal experience with Jesus Christ is profound, and receiving Him as Savior is life-altering. Every young person who had not made Jesus the Lord of their life left having been born of the Spirit. Those who hadn't received the baptism of the Holy Spirit were filled and spoke in tongues.

Such indescribable things happened that night, I find it difficult to explain. It had to be *experienced*.

The Desire to Share Our Experience

Once we were able to function, we wanted to tell what happened to us. No matter that it was almost midnight, such an incredible move of the Spirit had to be shared.

Some of the youth called their parents from the church phone, sobbing and praising God. Several church members without children were called too. In between sobs, they heard, "Come to the church right now! Jesus is here!" Not knowing what was happening and alarmed at the crying, everyone rushed to the church.

When parents and church members walked through the double doors, they were stunned. They were met with crying, dancing, and speaking in tongues.

The adults saw the results of God touching our souls. They witnessed the outward manifestation of what had just taken place in us. But they did not experience the inner transformation of a personal encounter with the Holy Spirit. How could they? They weren't there when God filled the church and His Spirit clothed us with His Presence.

At the Sunday night service following our encounter, we gave testimony to what happened. To give testimony is to present evidence of something you witnessed. We testified of salvation by the Name of Jesus. The Spirit was upon us as we preached, prayed, and prophesied in His Name. If the testimony of Jesus is the spirit of prophecy, we flowed in the spirit of prophecy that night. We were baptized in the Holy Spirit as Jesus prophesied in the book of Acts.

Do not leave Jerusalem, but wait for the gift the Father promised, which you have heard Me discuss. For John baptized with water, but in a few days you will be baptized with the Holy Spirit.

Acts 1:4-5

Young People Need God Encounters

Churches that set their children and youth aside and wait for them to reach maturity before being included in "real church" are missing one of the greatest potentials for revival. Youth are hungry to experience God and often search for the empowerment of the Holy Spirit. God notices and responds to hungry hearts. Young people who are truly touched by an encounter with God will never forget that event. And if they stray from Him later, they will return to their faith.

> Youth are hungry to experience God and often search for the empowerment of the Holy Spirit.

Even as a six-year-old child, I recognized the anointing of the Holy Spirit. One summer during vacation Bible school, I was sitting at a table in the church's fellowship hall gluing and pasting Bible characters when something startling happened. My grandmother was teaching the Bible lesson when I sensed

— 27 —

a change in her voice, and a Presence filled the room. When I looked up, she was crying.

"Kids, you have to ask Jesus to come into your hearts. You must be born again." We listened with rapt attention as my grandmother led us in a short prayer: "Jesus, come into my heart. You are my Savior." After repeating that prayer, I was filled with joy. I knew *something* had happened to me. After class, we had an opportunity to tell what happened to us at a testimony service. We were born of the Spirit, just as Jesus said!

Two years later, my sister, our pastor's daughter, and I had another supernatural encounter when we were baptized in the Holy Spirit.

Wildfire in the Beanfield

It was a Sunday afternoon in September, just before the soybean harvest. My sister Beverly, the pastor's daughter, and I were outside playing under the elm tree and enjoying the cooler weather when we began to talk about Jesus.

We had heard specific teaching on how to lead people to salvation through Jesus Christ in church the week before. My sister was five years old, I was eight, and the pastor's daughter was thirteen. We listened intently to the teaching and memorized the scriptures to use.

Around 4 o'clock that afternoon, we decided to take the lawn tractor, go across the farm to the nearest neighbor's house a half-mile away, and win them to Jesus.

Our neighbor had three children around our age. We had played with them a few times and found out they did not go to church.

We prepared and practiced saying the scriptures we were going to use.

There is none righteous, no, not one.

Romans 3:10 KJV

You must be born again.

John 3:7 ESV

If you confess with your mouth the Lord Jesus and believe in your heart that God has raised Him from the dead, you will be saved.

Romans 10:9 NKJV

All three of us got on the lawn tractor onto which Dad had welded an extra seat. We made our way down the turn row, which is a strip of uncropped land at the edge of the field. The lawn tractor made deep tracks in that sandy loam soil as we headed to our neighbor's house.

I stopped the tractor when it occurred to me that we had forgotten a very important step that we learned in the "personal evangelism" class.

"We forgot to pray," I said. "Let's go in the soybean field and pray for God to help us so they will be saved."

The dust flew as we tromped across the turn row and into the tall beans. This was a great place to pray. It was very private.

After stepping on the stalks and mashing down enough foliage to make a decent size "prayer room," we sat down in a circle. I led off in prayer: "Lord, we need Your help. Tell us what to say so they will want to be saved."

My sister and the pastor's daughter each said a prayer asking for various kinds of help in witnessing.

We had not finished our prayers when I heard the wind blowing from the north across the tops of the beans. It sort of sounded like wind blowing through the leaves of a sycamore tree—a rattling, shimmering noise, but then it became much louder as it roared closer to us.

Concerned about a storm, we peaked above the soybeans only to see what looked like fire racing across the tops of the beans. In a second, it hit us and knocked us flat on our backs.

I had been born again two years before but had not been filled with the Holy Spirit and spoken in tongues yet. Instantly, I was talking loudly in a language I did not know.

The pastor's daughter was lying on her back speaking in tongues. When we were able to sit up again, we were laughing, crying, and praising God!

My sister, however, was crying tears of sadness. When I asked what was wrong, she cried, "I'm not saved!"

Here was my opportunity to lead someone to Jesus!

"Just ask Him to come into your heart, and you will be saved." As soon as she said those words, she began speaking in a heavenly language, baptized in the Holy Spirit.

After a considerable amount of time had passed, I heard my mother's voice calling in the distance. It was time for the Sunday night service, so we got back on the lawn tractor and headed to the house with tears of joy running down our faces, all the while speaking in tongues.

My dear Pentecostal grandmother was standing in the yard with my mom. Both had worried looks on their faces when they saw we were crying. Something must have happened. Was someone hurt?

When we got near enough, they could hear us praising God and speaking in tongues. My grandmother began weeping and dancing in the Spirit, rejoicing at the outpouring of the Spirit upon us kids.

Over the years, my sister and I have talked about this experience in 1962 and the outpouring at the church in 1968. It is indelibly etched in our minds.

I acknowledge that these are unusual experiences, and most people receive the Holy Spirit without such demonstrations. Why us? I don't know.

Maybe the prayers of our ancestors reached out in time to the generation to come. Or maybe the anointing absorbed by those generations who attended the great tent meetings became part of our DNA?

Perhaps the simplest explanation is that God hears the prayers of children asking for help to witness, and that helper is the Holy Spirit. One thing I do know—these outpourings are not over, and there will be greater signs and wonders among the children and young people when the next wave comes.

> This new move of the Holy Spirit will include young children and teenagers who are fresh vessels for the Spirit, untainted by religious dogma but hungry for God.

The new is built upon the *old*. Time doesn't flow backward but forward. This new move of the Holy Spirit will include young children and teenagers who are fresh vessels for the Spirit, untainted by religious dogma but hungry for God.

CHAPTER 2

PREACHING IN THE POWER OF THE SPIRIT

The anointing from that service in 1968 lingered, and I preached my first sermon a few months later at my church. It was short, and I was worried. Would adults listen to a 14-year-old preaching? I guess it didn't matter because one of the adults responded to the salvation invitation I gave. One more person was born again into the Kingdom of God!

While studying and preparing for my sermon that week, I told God I was nervous and worried about adults listening to 1) a child and 2) a girl. I sought the Lord for direction and help. Without a concordance and before technology allowed internet searches, the Holy Spirit graciously sent me to Jeremiah 1.

> *The Lord said to me, "I knew you before you were formed within your mother's womb; before you were born I sanctified you and appointed you as my spokesman to the world."*
> *"O Lord God," I said, "I can't do that! I'm far too young! I'm only a youth!"*

*"Don't say that," he replied, "for you will go wher-
ever I send you and speak whatever I tell you to.
And don't be afraid of the people, for I, the Lord,
will be with you and see you through."*

*Then he touched my mouth and said, "See, I have
put my words in your mouth! Today your work
begins, to warn the nations and the kingdoms
of the world. In accord with my words spoken
through your mouth I will tear down some and
destroy them, and plant others, nurture them,
and make them strong and great."*

Jeremiah 1:4-10 TLB

I didn't comprehend the totality of God's call to Jeremiah.
But His Word to me through these verses was that I was called
by Him. And I should not be afraid of what the adults or anyone else would think of me, a youth and only a girl.

I knew I would grow to become an adult, and my concerns
about being young would pass. But I wondered if God made a
mistake.

The role of women in society and in the church at that time
was mostly a silent one as far as I had observed. If acceptance
of women was happening in the American culture in the late
1960s, it hadn't reached our small town! And then there was
that scripture Paul wrote about women keeping silent in the
church. I had already violated that verse!

No one in our family was a preacher, so I didn't know who
to ask about my dilemma. My dad was not a minister at that

time. He was a cotton farmer, as were all our extended family. Since there wasn't anyone to discuss this with, I was left to figure it out by myself.

Trying to Find My Place

Our denomination allowed women to preach. However, they were generally sent as missionaries to foreign countries where they killed you and ate you for dinner! I knew God had called me, but where?

I didn't know any female pastors, only missionaries. One woman I knew, my grandmother's friend, spoke at our church every once in a while. Although she was highly respected and obviously called to the ministry, I couldn't see myself in her shoes. There was her clothing for one thing. And then there was the guitar she slung over her shoulder before she started to preach loudly.

For a teenage girl, my grandmother's friend was a rather startling introduction to women in ministry. I could not personally identify with her or see myself ministering that way. Her style didn't quite fit and was not what I had imagined myself to be in serving God.

As a result, I stayed with the idea of going on missions trips and eventually preaching to people as a missionary. I made multiple trips to Mexico and South America in my teens with others from my denomination.

My itinerary also included Munich, Germany during the 1972 Olympics. I was looking forward to that trip until the

Spirit of God gave me a red light on going. Later, my parents and I were horrified as we watched the news reports. Terrorists had attacked and killed 11 members of the Israeli Olympic delegation.

I learned an important lesson when that happened. Yes, your mission may seem important—and witnessing for Jesus always is. But it is more important to follow the Holy Spirit's leading and be where He wants you to be. Sometimes that means *not going*, even if you are called.

In the book of Acts, Paul and his companions seemed to run into dead ends.

> It is more important to follow the Holy Spirit's leading and be where He wants you to be.

After the Holy Spirit had prevented them from speaking the word in the province of Asia, they traveled through the region of Phrygia and Galatia. And when they came to the border of Mysia, they tried to enter Bithynia, but the Spirit of Jesus would not permit them.

Acts 16:6-7

Paul later received specific direction from the Lord.

> *During the night, Paul had a vision of a man*
> *of Macedonia standing and pleading with him,*
> *"Come over to Macedonia and help us." As soon as*
> *Paul had seen the vision, we got ready to leave for*
> *Macedonia, concluding that God had called us to*
> *preach the gospel to them.*
>
> **Acts 16:9-10**

Sometimes the most difficult thing to do is sit still and not go.

Erroneous Thinking

Some things are now obvious to me as I look back with the knowledge of the scripture and many years of experience. Yet I see Christians wandering down the same erroneous path that I took.

First, I never was called to be a missionary. Missions was not in my heart. The only reason I decided my calling must be missions was that I couldn't think of anything else it could be. Through the process of elimination and based on culture and bias, I was left with the only calling my denomination deemed acceptable—a foreign missionary.

I highly respect the great men and women who have this special call to the nations of the world. But it was erroneous thinking to believe I was called to that office just because I couldn't think of anything else.

I ultimately discovered that God called me to remain in the United States to teach, preach, and write. I was called to do something that didn't exist and couldn't be defined in 1968.

Second, I was called before I was born, and God didn't make a mistake. Throughout history, other women have been called to the ministry. And the Holy Spirit made a way for them to accomplish their calling despite the prejudices of their times.

A member of my staff who was raised in the Catholic Church told me she felt God calling her one Sunday during mass. She rejected the nudging of the Holy Spirit because she was afraid it meant becoming a nun. That was the religious paradigm she lived in. In her mind, it was the only profession a call from God could possibly mean.

Denominations Shouldn't Define Your Calling

To allow a denomination to define your ministry is a tragedy. It often leads people with a true calling to occupy positions that are out of God's will. Some denominations only believe in the office of a pastor and an evangelist. But what do you do if your gift and anointing are that of a teacher?

"Sister, you can teach Sunday school. We appreciate anyone who will teach the children or young people." (These were acceptable areas for women to teach.) "Brother, you teach well. Would you take our adult Sunday school class?"

A lack of Bible understanding relegates the office of teacher to a secondary function rather than a divine appointment by God. (And God forbid if you are called to be a prophet in those denominations!)

The apostle Paul instructed the church at Ephesus that these appointments, callings, and offices are *gifts* to the body of Christ:

> *And [His gifts to the church were varied and] He Himself appointed some as apostles [special messengers, representatives], some as prophets [who speak a new message from God to the people], some as evangelists [who spread the good news of salvation], and some as pastors and teachers [to shepherd and guide and instruct].*

Ephesians 4:11 AMP

How I wish I had read this scripture with the revelation of the Holy Spirit and understanding. The idea that God could use me to speak as an anointed teacher, write books, and prophesy never occurred to me. I could have saved myself and others a lot of grief!

I will never forget my grandmother's tears when I announced I had committed my life to be a missionary. And I was willing to die for my faith—even if they killed me and ate me!

I think God honored my commitment to Him and of being willing to die. However, the dying part was not a revelation to my spirit. I was just *willing* to do whatever God wanted me to do.

Commitment to God and the Call

The concept of commitment is not taught much today. Nor is the prayer, "Not my will, but Your will be done." I hear Bible students (and ministers) announce that God called them to be a prophet. It sometimes sounds as though they think that office has the most power and honor. It appears that *they* chose it for themselves. Paul told the church at Corinth that a calling is an appointment given by God.

> *And in the church God has appointed first of all apostles, second prophets, third teachers, then workers of miracles, and those with gifts of healing, helping, administration, and various tongues.*

1 Corinthians 12:28

If God has called you, He will anoint you with the gifts and graces required to stand in that office. You may start out teaching Sunday school. When your anointing and gifts become obvious, your promotion will come from the Lord (see Ps. 75:6-7).

First Corinthians 12:28 lists other appointments that Paul did not mention in his letter to the Ephesians. They include gifts of healing, helping, administration, and various tongues. These are powerful gifts to the body of Christ and are needed for the full authority of the Church to become known. But these appointments are not usually emphasized within the church in general, i.e., in denominational, charismatic, Pentecostal, and other churches.

What are you called to? For the Church of Jesus Christ to function in the power of the Spirit, the entire body must be in the position they are called to. But if you don't know those positions exist, how will you be able to step into them?

> **When God calls, there are only two ways to answer: yes or no. He is not asking a multiple-choice question.**

Everyone who believes in Jesus is called and has a purpose and position in the body, whether they recognize it or not. Unfortunately, if a position is not emphasized and doesn't have a lot of bells and whistles, Christians don't believe their role is important.

People say things like, "I like to decorate, but the church doesn't need that." "The only thing I am good at is social media. I can't help." "I don't like to talk to people. I'm only good with numbers and accounting." Well? Don't you think the body of Christ needs these functions?

When God Calls

Our excuses can be endless. I thought I had a valid concern. In 1968, the church world as a whole (and society to an extent) did not accept or welcome women in ministry. But when God calls, there are only two ways to answer: yes or no. He is not asking a multiple-choice question.

Are you going to do what God told you to do or what the church world and society say is acceptable? Pushing against powerful tribal forces and opinions is not easy. Every day, we are told about our limitations, whether verbally or implied.

Those forces were at work during Jesus' time. Aside from religious and military oppression, classes of people were oppressed, including slaves and women. It was into this mix of society that Jesus declared:

> *The Spirit of the Lord is on Me, because He has anointed Me to preach good news to the poor. He has sent Me to proclaim liberty to the captives and recovery of sight to the blind, to release the oppressed, to proclaim the year of the Lord's favor.*

Luke 4:18-19

If we believe we are accomplishing anything in our ability, we are already on the wrong track and headed in the wrong direction.

Jesus proclaimed release from oppression. And the light of God in Him revealed a new concept for living free from all oppression.

Galatians 3:28 says, *"There is neither Jew nor Greek, slave nor free, male nor female, for you are all one in Christ Jesus."* When I discovered this verse, I was without excuse.

Unfortunately, it didn't seem as though the rest of the church had read it!

What was Paul talking about? He was referring to our spirit and our equality in the Holy Spirit. The forces and opinions of the physical world do not prevent us from functioning and accomplishing equally in the realm of the spirit and the Kingdom of God.

If we believe we are accomplishing anything in our ability, we are already on the wrong track and headed in the wrong direction. The works of God are accomplished by the Spirit. We may speak the Word, but the Holy Spirit activates and energizes that Word to bring about the result. Our responsibility is to speak and do what God says and leave the results to Him.

CHAPTER 3

LEARNING TO FLOW

As a young Christian, the only gifts of the Spirit I knew about were tongues and interpretation. I knew when someone spoke out in the gift of tongues, they were speaking in an unknown language. Sometimes it was a heavenly language, and sometimes it was an earthly language the person had not learned.

After someone speaks out in tongues in a language they *do not* know, the Holy Spirit gives the interpretation to somebody else to be delivered to those present. That person is supernaturally given the understanding of what was said. They then speak out the interpretation of the tongue in a language they *do* understand.

The first time I received an interpretation of tongues was on a Sunday morning in my church. My eyes were closed because we were taught to be very reverent when the Holy Spirit moved on someone to speak out in tongues. We all bowed our heads and closed our eyes in reverence.

(Later, I came to realize that you can be reverent in your heart whether you're standing, sitting, or even lying down.)

But that day when a woman in our church gave the tongues, words suddenly started coming to me. I actually saw the words. I saw what looked like a newspaper and watched as words were typed out across it in my mind's eye. I read each word as it was typed.

"For the Lord says, 'If you will worship and praise Me, you will see that I will move in your midst.'"

"Well," I thought. "That's the strangest thing that's ever happened to me." Later that week, my dad and I were in his truck driving to the farm to check on the irrigation wells, and I asked him about what happened.

"When somebody speaks out in tongues," I asked, "do you understand what the person is saying?"

"Yes," he said. "As the person is talking, words come to me down on the inside."

"Well, I see the words like a newspaper headline."

First Corinthians 12:6 says, *"there are diversities of operations"* (KJV). That simply means people operate in different ways when they are used in the gifts.

My dad was used a lot in tongues and interpretation of tongues. However, he never saw words being typed in a headline style. I *saw* words, but he *heard* words. Most people receive the words in their spirit when they are given the interpretation. But that's not the only way to receive the interpretation of tongues.

Sometimes when someone spoke in tongues, the interpretation came to me in an outline form. I would see Topic Number 1 and then a), b), c) underneath it. I read through the outline, and the Holy Spirit filled in the gaps. The words just rolled out of me as I gave the interpretation.

Different Ways of Working

There are different gifts, but the same Spirit. There are different ministries, but the same Lord. There are different ways of working, but the same God works all things in all people.

1 Corinthians 12:4-6

We see in verse 7 that the gifts are manifestations of the Holy Spirit. And the Holy Spirit manifests Himself in nine ways.

To each is given the manifestation of the Spirit for the common good. For to one is given through the Spirit the utterance of wisdom, and to another the utterance of knowledge according to the same Spirit, to another faith by the same Spirit, to another gifts of healing by the one Spirit, to another the working of miracles, to another prophecy, to another the ability to distinguish between spirits, to another various kinds of tongues, to another the interpretation of tongues. All these are empowered by one and the same Spirit, who apportions to each one individually as he wills.

1 Corinthians 12:7-11 ESV

The word of knowledge can come as a revelation to your spirit, or you might have a vision. But just because the gifts of the Spirit operate one way in somebody doesn't mean that is the only way they operate.

There are essential, basic truths about the gifts of the Spirit that are true in definition as to their purpose. But they flow differently depending upon the person the gift flows through.

Verse 9 of First Corinthians 12 lists "gifts of healing" as one of the nine gifts. In Greek, both words are plural: "gifts of healings."

I have noticed that some ministers are specifically used in certain areas of healing. Some people are anointed to minister healing in deafness. Anytime they lay their hands on someone who can't hear, the deaf ear instantly opens. For them, almost 100 percent of the people are healed of deafness. But they don't have that same rate of success in other areas.

Then I've seen others who were anointed with gifts of healings in the area of tumors and growths. Almost without fail, growths disappeared when they laid their hands on someone afflicted that way.

The Gift of Prophecy

Of the nine gifts of the Spirit, three are called utterance gifts— meaning that they are spoken. The utterance gifts include tongues, interpretation of tongues, and prophecy.

Growing up, I didn't know anything about prophecy. I thought it was something Ezekiel and Daniel did. I didn't realize it was a gift that could be used in a church service or prayer group.

I went to a Pentecostal Bible college and thought, "What better way to find out about the gifts of the Spirit than at Bible school?" But after I settled in, I found out they didn't know any more about spiritual gifts than I did. But thank God we have the Holy Spirit as our teacher. While at school, the Holy Spirit began to move and operate through me in spite of my ignorance.

Once a week in our college dormitories, each floor met at the end of the hall to pray. I was sitting cross-legged on the floor worshiping the Lord when words started coming to me. Sometimes they came to my spirit, and sometimes I saw them the same way the interpretation of tongues had manifested in me.

However, the anointing would come on me *before* some-body spoke out in tongues. When that happened, I prayed, "O God, please hurry and have someone speak in tongues so I can give this out."

I didn't know you could give a word without tongues. Finally, somebody would speak a few words in tongues. It really wasn't a message in tongues. They were just speaking a few praise words in their heavenly language. But I would be so relieved that I could finally give out the word I received from the Holy Spirit.

At spring break, I drove home to visit my family and told my dad that it was hard to wait for a message in tongues to be given when I already had the English words. He laughed and said, "That's not the gift of interpretation; that's the gift of prophecy. You don't have to wait for tongues. Just speak the words out in English."

Until then, I didn't know that tongues plus interpretation were the equivalent of the gift of prophecy. I thought I couldn't give a word out until someone spoke in tongues. But a word of prophecy can be given on its own without someone speaking in tongues first.

Covet to Prophesy

Wherefore, brethren, covet to prophesy, and forbid not to speak with tongues. Let all things be done decently and in order.

1 Corinthians 14:39-40 KJV

The apostle Paul told us to *"covet to prophesy." Covet* means "earnestly desire." If he said to covet, there must be something more valuable about prophecy than what we thought. Notice what Paul didn't say: "Now, the Holy Spirit may give some people the gift of prophecy. If He does, you might want to operate in it." No, Paul tells us to *covet*. Why would he use a strong word like that?

First, I believe the gift of prophecy is supernatural, as are all the nine gifts of the Spirit. They are not human abilities or talents. The gift of the word of knowledge is not somebody who has read a lot of books. The gift of the word of wisdom is not somebody who has a lot of wisdom. These gifts are supernaturally imparted.

I want to operate in the supernatural, don't you? So a good reason to covet to prophesy is that we desire the supernatural, and prophecy is supernatural.

Second, prophecy deals with words. You're dealing with words and their power, their significance, and their effect. That is how God operates. He *spoke* the worlds into existence.

Words release power onto the earth. They release ideas and concepts to the minds and hearts of those who hear the word of the prophecy. It could be encouragement or comfort.

The most potent effect of prophecy is that words are containers that carry the speaker's essence, energy, and intent. When God speaks, it is a *living* word that will accomplish His purpose. Words anointed by the Holy Spirit release the energy of God upon the earth.

> **Words anointed by the Holy Spirit release the energy of God upon the earth.**

Third, prophecy is a vehicle through which other spiritual gifts can be delivered. Prophecy can contain a word of wisdom, and gifts of healings can be carried through a prophetic word.

Prophecy combined with the word of wisdom could bring supernatural knowledge of what will take place in the future. It could be forthtelling or foretelling events that will take place. If prophecy is combined with the word of knowledge, it would reveal an event or action taking place now or in the past.

Paul gave us these instructions: *"Despise not prophesy-ing. Prove all things; hold fast that which is good"* (1 Thess. 5:20-21 KJV). He's telling us to test and prove all prophecy, but don't despise it when someone gives something that's not from God or is of their own making. Some people miss it when they prophesy. But the true gift of prophecy manifested by the Spirit of God is powerful.

We've all had something go wrong with our cars. But when they didn't function properly, we never quit using them. No one would do that.

We can be so smart in the natural but very dull when it comes to the realm of the spirit. Just because the gift of proph-ecy is misused or doesn't operate properly is no reason not to use it or refuse to listen to another prophecy. We are learning and mistakes happen. But anyone can be taught the proper expression of this gift.

Secrets Manifested Through Prophecy

At one time, I thought believers were mature in the gift of prophecy. After all, the utterance gifts have been operating for quite a while in the church—almost everybody can prophesy. But there are areas of prophecy that we haven't tapped into yet. Paul says something interesting about it.

> *Thus tongues are a sign not for believers but for unbelievers, while prophecy is a sign not for unbe-lievers but for believers. If, therefore, the whole church comes together and all speak in tongues,*

and outsiders or unbelievers enter, will they not say that you are out of your minds? But if all prophesy, and an unbeliever or outsider enters, he is convicted by all, he is called to account by all, the secrets of his heart are disclosed, and so, falling on his face, he will worship God and declare that God is really among you.

1 Corinthians 14:22-25 ESV

Have you ever seen the gift of prophecy operate during a church service, and unbelievers are convicted and judged? That the secrets of their hearts were exposed, and they fell on their face in worship to God? Have you ever seen the prophetic in operation that powerfully?

I have not personally seen this, but Paul indicated that it would happen. If it took place in his day, it should happen today. It has happened somewhat.

I heard Kenneth E. Hagin tell about a service he was conducting in a church when the spirit of prophecy came upon him. He heard himself say under the anointing to a tall man in the back of the church, "You said, 'I don't believe what the preacher is saying. I don't believe a word of it! But just to please you, I'll go to church with you.'"

Hagin said before he finished prophesying, the man ran to the altar under the conviction of the Holy Spirit and was saved and filled with the Holy Spirit. The man told Hagin, "That's exactly what I said!"

I've also read books in which these things have occurred. When the true spirit of prophecy is operating, we will see this happen more and more. We can't believe we are mature in prophetic gifts until we see that.

Seek to Excel

I've concluded that we don't know as much about the spirit of prophecy as we need to. Paul said, *"Since you are eager for manifestations of the Spirit, strive to excel in building up the church"* (1 Cor. 14:12 ESV).

I challenge you to covet to prophesy; don't despise it. If you haven't already, allow the spirit of prophecy to begin operating in you when you're praying or even singing in the shower. As you allow the manifestation of the Spirit to come upon you, you will become more sensitive to both the gifts of the Holy Spirit and His leading in your life.

CHAPTER 4

THE SPIRIT OF PROPHECY IN PRAYER

First Corinthians 14:3 gives us a definition of what prophecy is supposed to do: "*But he that prophesieth speaketh unto men to edification, and exhortation, and comfort*" (KJV). A prophetic word is not a truly inspired utterance if it doesn't edify, exhort, or comfort.

Edify means to build up. The word *exhortation* gives the idea of encouragement, which we all need from time to time. And *comfort* brings consolation and reassurance. It cheers someone up. This type of prophecy is speaking to believers in a group setting.

Prophecy is speaking words that are inspired by the Holy Spirit in a language you know. It can be given in private prayer or a private conversation or in a group setting.

On many occasions, I have prayed prophetically under the anointing of the spirit of prophecy when I was alone and interceding for others. As I prayed and yielded to the Holy Spirit, He took over, and my words took on a deeper meaning. I began saying things that didn't come from my mind. If I tried to think it out beforehand and pray that kind of prayer, I wouldn't be able to come up with what I prayed.

Praying prophetically (and giving a prophecy) does not come from your natural thinking. You begin to pray under the inspiration and utterance of the Holy Spirit. You're not thinking things like, "God bless so and so." Or "God help our church." "God do this; God do that."

Oral Roberts once told my dad that he prayed in tongues and then interpreted his prayers in English to receive God's wisdom and direction for his ministry and the building of the ORU campus.

Since tongues plus interpretation is equivalent to the simple gift of prophecy, praying under the anointing of prophecy produces the same results.

Intercession for My Sister

I remember an incident that took place while I was ministering at a conference in California. As I was visiting with other ministers, suddenly I was overcome with the feeling that something was terribly wrong. I excused myself and went to my motel room and literally threw myself across the bed, interceding in tongues by the Spirit.

After about 45 minutes, I stood up and began to declare the covering of the blood of Jesus, Psalm 91, and that no weapon formed against my sister, Beverly, and her family would prosper. I was startled to hear this come out of my mouth because I did not know who I was praying for until then.

I immediately called my mom and asked if she knew where Beverly was. My sister had just called my mother crying. She and her three children were driving in the car when a terrible accident happened right in front of them. They narrowly missed being in it. One of the cars caught on fire, resulting in multiple deaths, but my sister and her children were unharmed.

Paul's Prayers

Ephesians 1 and 3 and Colossians 1 record the prayers of Paul. While attending Rhema Bible Training College, I heard Kenneth E. Hagin say that he was amazed at the revelation that came to him after he began praying Paul's prayers. So I started praying those prayers myself. After a while, I noticed that my prayers took on a prophetic element.

My daily prayer was: "Father, I pray that You would give unto me the spirit of wisdom and revelation in the knowledge of Christ. I ask that the eyes of my understanding would be enlightened. I want to know what the hope of my calling is and what the riches of the glory of Your inheritance in the saints are. And what is the exceeding greatness of Your power toward me because I believe according to the working of Your mighty power, which You wrought in Christ when you raised Him from the dead and set Him at Your right hand in the heavenly places, far above all principality and power and might and dominion and every name that is named, not only in this world but also in that which is to come." (Taken from Ephesians 1:17-21.)

The Ephesians' prayers were written under the inspiration of the Spirit of God. When you pray them aloud, you tap into the same spirit of prophecy that operated in Paul when he prayed them.

> Words vibrate with frequency. When they are anointed by the Holy Spirit, they transform the surroundings by the energy of God.

One day when I got to the end of that prayer, the prayer stopped, but the Holy Ghost kept going. And I prayed under the spirit of prophecy.

I prayed, "Father, I pray in the Name of Jesus that the entire body of Christ would come into the full knowledge of Christ. That the entire body of Christ would walk in the wealth of the eternities."

I heard words coming out of me that I didn't know I knew. When you begin to pray in the spirit of prophecy, your words become alive, operative, energizing, quick, and powerful. They affect everything around you.

Words vibrate with frequency. When they are anointed by the Holy Spirit, they transform the surroundings by the energy of God.

What to Pray?

Some people say it's hard for them to pray because they don't know what to say. When you don't know how to pray, pray in tongues. Romans 8:26-27 says:

> *In the same way, the Spirit helps us in our weakness. For we do not know how we ought to pray, but the Spirit Himself intercedes for us with groans too deep for words. And He who searches our hearts knows the mind of the Spirit, because the Spirit intercedes for the saints according to the will of God.*

As you pray in tongues, expect to receive the interpretation of what you are praying.

Prayer can seem like hard work. I liken it to plowing behind a mule. But when the spirit of prophecy comes upon you in prayer, it breaks up the ground like you are using a John Deere tractor. Hard ground is no match for a tractor! What you are praying about is taken care of easily. When you learn to pray with the Holy Spirit, He makes it easy for you.

Corporate Prayer

The spirit of prophecy also flows in corporate prayer. We read how God used Peter and John to heal a lame man in Acts 3:6. Peter spoke anointed, God-energized words: *"In the Name of Jesus Christ the Nazarene, get up and walk!"* (NLT). Then acting in faith, he pulled the lame man off the ground and to his feet.

Peter then preached to the crowd that gathered, and 5,000 people believed in Jesus. The two apostles were arrested and questioned by the chief priests and elders. When they were released, they were commanded not to speak or teach in the Name of Jesus.

> I practice *connecting my mouth to my spirit* by praying in tongues.

And being let go, they went to their own company, and reported all that the chief priests and elders had said unto them. And when they heard that, they lifted up their voice to God with one accord.

Acts 4:23-24 KJV

The early church gathered together and prayed with *one voice* unto the Lord. I've often tried to figure out how the entire church could have prayed one prayer. Did they write down the prayer on sheets of paper and pass it out to everyone? Did the leaders say, "Now, let's all together pray this prayer?"

No. I believe the spirit of prophecy moved upon that entire church. And when the Spirit of God moves upon a body of believers, everyone will *say the same thing.*

That body of believers prayed the same inspired words. And after they did, scripture says, *"the place was shaken where they were assembled together"* (Acts 4:31 KJV). That is a mighty manifestation of the spirit of prophecy.

The Spirit of Prophecy in Intercession

There is an element of prophecy in intercession. You see that in the books of Jeremiah and Lamentations. When Jeremiah cried out to God, the spirit of prophecy guided his words.

During intercession, the spirit of prophecy can come upon you. When it does, it's as if you are grieving, but then the spirit of prophecy takes over. And God expresses Himself through your intercession. This type of prayer is inspired and anointed.

That has happened to me during intercession. The spirit of prophecy suddenly came on me, and it was powerful. And I saw the effect of what was prayed about for the person or situation I was interceding about.

The Spirit of Prophecy in Preaching

An element of prophecy can come forth while you are preaching. At times while I am ministering, I hear myself say things I never thought of before. I wonder how I knew what I just said. I didn't, but the Spirit of God did. When that happens, words come to my spirit, not my mind.

(I practice *connecting my mouth to my spirit* by praying in tongues. The more I pray in tongues, the more sensitive I am to what the Spirit wants to say.)

As you listen to a minister, you can tell when the spirit of prophecy comes upon them. As they are ministering, you will hear a difference in their voice and what they say. They switch over into a stronger anointing, and it sounds like something was added to their words. That is an element of prophecy.

When the spirit of prophecy comes upon me, it seems as though I entered a cloud and am watching myself speak. It feels like I am totally removed from the equation because the Spirit of God is in control. I gave Him control because I yielded myself to the anointing.

CHAPTER 5

THE SPIRIT OF PROPHECY IN MUSIC

Some of the most amazing flows of music I have witnessed were in the early Kenneth E. Hagin Campmeeting services. Brother Hagin would be given a message from God. At certain times during the service, he would turn to his son-in-law, Buddy Harrison, and ask if he had something in the Spirit.

Out would come an original psalm or spiritual song that literally "hit the spot" and further enhanced the prophetic anointing on Brother Hagin.

In one service, Brother Hagin called upon Vicki Jamison Peterson, who launched out in the Spirit with "He's More Than Enough." Anyone in that meeting will be able to recall the unusual high-intensity anointing that washed over the whole crowd as she sang this *new song* in the Spirit.

It remains one of my favorite songs, and just hearing it in my mind brings that same anointing and Presence of God that manifested during that service.

Anointed Musicians

I believe God wants us to enter into these deeper realms of the spirit in song and music. In some church services, the music is approached as if it's just something to do before the minister starts preaching—have a song service. If we approach worship that way, we don't understand its true purpose.

When the spirit of prophecy operates during worship, our praise to God reaches a higher level. Instead of singing songs to get the congregation in the mood to listen to the Word, the spirit of prophecy creates a completely different atmosphere.

Worship becomes prophetic.

Worship lifts the congregation to the heavenly places in Christ. Instead of words being mouthed, worship becomes prophetic. It edifies, exhorts, and comforts and pulls us to the heavenlies.

When we reach the heavenly places during worship, we put ourselves in a position where the Spirit can sweep through the congregation and minister to everyone in attendance.

I wonder how many times the Holy Spirit is grieved because people in the congregation need healing and need deliverance, but He is not allowed to move as He wants. The service consists of two or three songs, but the people never enter into worship. The minister preaches the sermon, takes up the offering, and everyone goes home. And many people are left in the same position as when they walked in.

When God's Spirit is present and able to move, it transforms us. People battling sickness can be healed in the presence of the Healer and through the gifts of healings. A person could fail to receive their healing by not believing in or accepting God's healing power. But no one can come that close to the Presence and power of God without the opportunity to receive His healing power. God is light and love, and darkness of any kind has to flee from His Presence.

> When the prophetic anointing of God is on the musicians, they will lead us to that place where God can work.

God inhabits the praise of His people. His Presence manifests when people truly worship Him. But singing songs *about* Him is not the same as worshiping Him for who He is. Singing about what He has done is a great testimony and brings an emotional response. But worship brings a spiritual response that magnifies God and puts Him first.

When the prophetic anointing of God is on the musicians, they will lead us to that place where God can work, where Jesus can minister, and where the Spirit of God can sweep through a congregation and not one person is left sick. Not one! I believe that will happen.

People will be supernaturally healed by being saturated with God's Presence and because they had an encounter with the Presence of our Lord and Savior, Jesus.

When we—the body of Christ—release the musicians to lead us into those places, we will see greater manifestations of the Spirit in signs and wonders.

One Voice

God can move in mighty ways when the Church is united in one voice. Look what happened in the following two situations when people came to God, not as many individual voices but as one sound.

> *And when the trumpeters and singers were joined in unison, making one sound to be heard in praising and thanking the Lord, and when they lifted up their voice with the trumpets and cymbals and other instruments for song and praised the Lord, saying, For He is good, for His mercy and loving-kindness endure forever, then the house of the Lord was filled with a cloud, so that the priests could not stand to minister because of the cloud, for the glory of the Lord filled the house of God.*

> **2 Chronicles 5:13-14 AMPC**

Notice that verse 13 says that the "trumpeters and singers were in unison making one sound." I have seen this happen to a great degree in the 1970s and some in the 1980s outpouring.

As the Spirit moved, the congregation would break forth in spontaneous singing in the language of the Spirit. With no direction from anyone but the Spirit, a beautiful melody was formed by groups of believers harmonizing, volume rising and falling as though directed by an unseen conductor. It was truly a heavenly experience!

In this outpouring of the Spirit, Spirit-filled believers will become so attuned to the Spirit of God that entire congregations will simultaneously sing the same song in the Spirit in the same language. They will make one sound unto the Lord in unison. And the glory of God will fill the place. It will be earth-shattering—the vibrational frequencies will resonate through the entire earth and shatter and destroy the enemy's plans.

> **The vibrational frequencies will resonate through the entire earth and shatter and destroy the enemy's plans.**

In this second example, many years had passed after the Temple in Jerusalem was dedicated. Three nations joined together to attack God's people. But instead of the king sending his best *soldiers* to lead the battle, King Jehoshaphat put his best *worshipers* in front of the army.

> *And they rose early in the morning and went out into the Wilderness of Tekoa; and as they went*

out, Jehoshaphat stood and said, Hear me, O Judah, and you inhabitants of Jerusalem! Believe in the Lord your God and you shall be established; believe and remain steadfast to His prophets and you shall prosper.

*When he had consulted with the people, he appointed singers to sing to the Lord and praise Him in their holy [priestly] garments as they went out before the army, saying, **Give thanks to the Lord, for His mercy and loving-kindness endure forever!***

2 Chronicles 20:20-21 AMPC

Notice the last verse in this passage. The people didn't say that God is a God of judgment or that He will strike and kill their enemies. No, they gathered together saying, "For the Lord is good and His mercy endureth forever."

Anointed Singing Defeats the Enemy

Look at what happened when they stood united and sang in unison.

And when they began to sing and to praise, the Lord set ambushments against the men of Ammon, Moab, and Mount Seir who had come against Judah, and they were [self-] slaughtered; for [suspecting betrayal] the men of Ammon and Moab rose against those of Mount Seir, utterly

*destroying them. And when they had made an end
of the men of Seir, they all helped to destroy one
another.*

2 Chronicles 20:22-23 AMPC

God anointed the musicians so powerfully that it ruined the
enemy. Because of the anointing upon them, God set ambushments against Israel's enemies, and they destroyed each other.

Anointed worship is one thing the devil cannot stand. He
won't stay around long when people enter into the high praises
of God.

There are songs given by the Spirit that will cause discouragement and depression to flee from your life. When the enemy
comes against you, singing praise will turn the tide. Certain
songs and musicians will resonate with you. And when discouragement comes, you must force yourself to sing these songs.

Personally, I have two or three songs that always lift me
up in praise and cause the battle to turn in my favor. Most of
these are songs of scripture set to music. One that I keep in my
heart is "Garment of Praise" by David Ingles. Brother Ingles
received his songs by the Spirit, often in Kenneth E. Hagin's
Campmeeting.

Put on the garment of praise
For the spirit of heaviness
Lift up your voice to God.
Praise with the Spirit
And the understanding
Oh, magnify the Lord.[1]

When you sing the praise of God out loud, you are making a statement of faith, and the anointing on God's Word sets a fire in your heart. Discouragement and depression must depart.

There is a rhythm, timing, and pattern of a song that will dispel darkness and release victory. The sound frequency of anointed words sung from the heart can resonate and change you from defeat to victory.

Music Sets the Stage for What God Can Do

It's time for the Spirit of God to be manifested more powerfully through songs and music. Intercession must be made for the musicians the same way we intercede for the pastor. We need to pray that the musicians reach places in the spirit and bring the entire congregation with them.

> There is a rhythm, timing, and pattern of a song that will dispel darkness and release victory.

When the congregation reaches the "heavenly places in Christ Jesus" and the preacher comes up to minister, it's like striking a match and setting a Holy Spirit fire in them. They are released and set free! When the spirit of prophecy has already been operating through the musicians, it is unleashed on the preacher and enables them to minister with a heightened sensitivity to the Spirit.

Singing and worshiping under the spirit of prophecy raises the entire congregation to a higher level. And it's sure a whole lot easier to minister! We need to contend for that. It's vital that we pray, believe, and expect God to manifest Himself in the music ministry.

Psalms, Hymns, and Spiritual Songs

Colossians 3:16 says, *"Let the word of Christ dwell in you richly in all wisdom; teaching and admonishing one another in psalms and hymns and spiritual songs, singing with grace in your hearts to the Lord"* (KJV).

This verse shows us that there are different kinds of songs. A psalm, or *psalmos* in Greek, is a sacred song sung to musical accompaniment. There's nothing wrong with singing the songs we have written. But are they sacred?

Hymns are songs of praise addressed to God. But have you ever noticed that most of our songs aren't addressed to Him? They are about God, what He has done, and how we feel about Him. But often, they are not addressed to Him.

One song that is addressed to God is "Thou Art Worthy." When we sing that song, we are worshiping God. We are addressing Him, not the audience. And that brings Him into our midst, and His Presence and glory manifest among us.

An entirely different anointing is upon that song than on other songs. I have never sung "Thou Art Worthy" and failed to see the anointing manifest.

Praise songs are sung about what God has *done*, often what He has done *for* us. Worship songs are adoring Him for who He *is*.

A spiritual song is a song of the Spirit and is revealed by the Holy Spirit. Don't you think that He knows the best way to praise God? When you hear a true song of the Spirit, it excites your spirit and lifts you up. An anointing is on it that paves the way for other gifts of the Spirit to manifest.

A woman who was mightily used in the area of spiritual songs was Vicki Jamison Peterson. She went home to be with the Lord in 2008. While she ministered, the Spirit of God gave her songs that she sang out under the anointing. She often sang out healings to people. Her ministry gift was a combination of the gift of prophecy in song, the gifts of healings, and the word of knowledge—the Spirit of God revealed who was being healed of specific sicknesses. The Spirit gave her not only the words to sing but also the melodies.

Her ministry was one of the most unusual and powerful that I have ever witnessed. One time Vicki told me that the anointing was ten times stronger in the area of healing when she *sang* the healings rather than when she *spoke* them.

The next time you are in a service, listen to what you are singing. It will show you what direction the service will go.

Vast Frontiers Ahead of Us

I believe vast frontier lands are ahead of us in the spirit realm, and we have not yet touched them. So many times people hear the Word being taught, and they think, "I've got it." But the more I learn, the more I realize that we don't "have it." We've barely gotten into what the Spirit wants to show us and do through us.

In 1981, I ministered along these lines at Dr. Lydia Berkey's church in Broken Arrow, Oklahoma. Dr. Berkey was an ordained minister with the Foursquare Gospel denomination. She attended Life Bible College while Aimee Semple McPherson was at the height of her ministry. At the end of the service, this prophetic word came from the Spirit of God through me.

> There are vast frontier lands in the spirit that are yet to be discovered. There are vast frontier lands in the spirit that God has laid out for you to discover. There are vast frontier lands in the spirit, and I alone know the way. These frontier lands are waiting for you to push into and take steps into that area of discovery. For the Spirit of God will take you higher, and He will take you beyond the things you now know. And He will take you beyond the things you have yet to experience. For there are frontier lands full of the things of God that you don't have any knowledge of. So take your liberty and enter in. Come with Me, and together we will discover what I have prepared for you.

We're going to spend eternity discovering the things of God. I want to get started now, don't you?

NOTE

1. "Garment of Praise" © 1976 David Ingles Music SESAC.
   Used by Permission

CHAPTER 6

PROPHETS AND THE MUSIC MINISTRY

In the Old Testament, prophets and musicians worked hand in hand. When the musician got in the Spirit through the music, so did the prophet. The musician created a portal to the Presence of God. By creating this opening to the heavenly realm, the power and wisdom of Almighty God would come upon the prophet.

In First Samuel 10, after the prophet Samuel anointed Saul to be king of Israel, he told Saul, *"You will come to the hill of God, where the garrison of the Philistines is; and when you come to the city, you will meet a company of prophets coming down from the high place with harp, tambourine, flute, and lyre before them, prophesying"* (1 Sam. 10:5 AMPC).

Notice carefully, in front of the prophets were musicians who had various instruments. Each instrument expressed a different vibration and state of worship to God.

The tambourine expressed joy and rejoicing. The harp resonated deep stirrings from the heart, and the flute was lilting and

> When the musician got in the Spirit through the music, so did the prophet. The musician created a portal to the Presence of God.

flowing in conversation with a holy God. As the musicians led the company while playing their instruments, the prophets prophesied.

The spirit of prophecy came upon the musicians, and because the anointing was on them, it flowed over onto the prophets. When the spirit of prophecy comes forth, the prophets prophesy as the musicians minister unto the Lord.

It's not happenstance that the prophets and musicians were together. The prophets put the musicians in front of them because they knew the music would stir up the gift of prophecy. The anointing would overflow onto them, and they would prophesy.

Verse 6 says, *"Then the Spirit of the Lord will come upon you mightily, and you will show yourself to be a prophet with them; and you will be turned into another man"* (AMPC). The spirit of prophecy flowing through the prophets turned Saul into another man. When he came under that anointing, he began to prophesy too.

If this were the only incident in the Bible where prophets called for a musician, we might say this incident with Saul was a coincidence, but it's not.

Three Kings Who Needed a Word

Another example of a prophet calling for a minstrel is found in Second Kings 3. Three kings had joined together to wage war against the King of Moab. They took a roundabout way through the wilderness to battle the Moabites. After seven days, they ran out of water for the army and the animals. One of the kings wanted to get God's mind on the matter.

> *But Jehoshaphat said, Is there no prophet of the Lord here by whom we may inquire of the Lord? One of the king of Israel's servants answered, Elisha son of Shaphat, who served Elijah, is here. Jehoshaphat said, The word of the Lord is with him. So Joram king of Israel and Jehoshaphat and the king of Edom went down to Elisha.*
>
> **2 Kings 3:11-12 AMPC**

Elisha was not pleased when he saw the kings. He didn't want to help the king of Israel because his parents were the wicked Ahab and Jezebel. But he said:

> *As the Lord of hosts lives, before Whom I stand, surely, were it not that I respect the presence of Jehoshaphat king of Judah, I would neither look at you nor see you [King Joram]. But now bring me a minstrel. And while the minstrel played, the hand and power of the Lord came upon [Elisha].*
>
> **2 Kings 3:14-15 AMPC**

The spirit of prophecy manifested while the minstrel played, and Elisha gave them God's word on what to do. Because they sought God, they were victorious in their battle against the Moabites. What do you think would have happened if they didn't have a musician?

Elisha needed the Spirit of God to come upon him before he received supernatural insight and wisdom. The great prophet could not turn his prophetic gift "on" whenever he wanted to.

The music moved Elisha into union with God—his heart and God's heart joined together, and a marvelous plan was revealed.

> **The great prophet could not turn his prophetic gift "on" whenever he wanted to.**

And he said, Thus says the Lord: Make this [dry] brook bed full of trenches.

For thus says the Lord: You shall not see wind or rain, yet that ravine shall be filled with water, so you, your cattle, and your beasts [of burden] may drink.

This is but a light thing in the sight of the Lord. He will deliver the Moabites also into your hands.

You shall smite every fenced city and every choice city, and shall fell every good tree and stop all

*wells of water and mar every good piece of land
with stones.*

*In the morning, when the sacrifice was offered,
behold, there came water by the way of Edom, and
the country was filled with water.*

2 Kings 3:16-20 AMPC

The early morning sun reflecting on the water made it look
like blood. When the Moabites saw the water, they thought it
was the blood of their enemies, so they rushed to take the spoil
and were defeated by the Israelites!

This miracle came from the Spirit of God through a musician to a prophet. Never underestimate the power of anointed
music.

Praise, Prophecy, and the Glory of God

In First Chronicles 25, we see how King David separated some
of the priests to temple service *"who should prophesy [being
inspired] with lyres, harps, and cymbals"* (1 Chron. 25:1
AMPC).

Verse 2 lists the sons of Asaph who *"prophesied (witnessed
and testified under divine inspiration) in keeping with the
king's order."* Verse 3 goes on to list the sons of Jeduthun
who prophesied *"under divine inspiration with the lyre in
thanksgiving and praise to the Lord."* We then see in verse
7 that 288 priests were trained and skillful in the songs of the
Lord.

David appointed 4,000 men to minister to the Lord in songs of praise and to prophesy. Let me ask you a question. If we had 4,000 people in a meeting who ministered to the Lord in praise, worship, and prophecy, what kind of service do you think we would have? Amazing, don't you think? Imagine how God would manifest Himself!

The following verses show how these Old Testament worshipers united in worship to make one sound in their praise to God.

> *And all the Levites who were singers—all of those of Asaph, Heman, and Jeduthun, with their sons and kinsmen, arrayed in fine linen, having cymbals, harps, and lyres—stood at the east end of the altar, and with them 120 priests blowing trumpets; and when the trumpeters and singers were joined in unison, making one sound to be heard in praising and thanking the Lord, and when they lifted up their voice with the trumpets and cymbals and other instruments for song and praised the Lord, saying, For He is good, for His mercy and loving-kindness endure forever, then the house of the Lord was filled with a cloud, so that the priests could not stand to minister because of the cloud, for the glory of the Lord filled the house of God.*

2 Chronicles 5:12-14 AMPC

The Song Calls You and Writes Itself

I had an amazing experience at a Native American drumming. It was not a ceremony per se but a lesson to teach drumming. Although my words are inadequate to describe a drumming, and I am not qualified to discuss this tradition, it was a very spiritual exercise.

Five of us sat around a large drum. The purpose of a drumming is to unite people, so the drumbeats must be in perfect timing. The song of the drum—i.e., the rhythm and beat—we were being taught was specific.

I have a pretty good sense of rhythm, but I noticed that I would be "off" a beat at one place in the drumming. After a couple times of missing the beat, I asked the Native teacher what I was doing wrong.

"Oh nothing," he said. "That is the song itself. No matter who plays it or how hard you try, the drum and the song have chosen that beat to be different."

What a thought! We are instruments to sing God's songs, and His songs sing (or play) themselves through us!

We don't choose to create songs or write music. The songs and the music seek and find the vessel of expression.

Frequency of Sound

The following is a word given by the Spirit by one of my staff members following my message on the spirit of prophecy in 1981.

Sound frequency is a key that opens the flood-gates of certain prophetic winds. Prophecy contains words from the Father's heart that He wants to be expressed on the earth. Imagine a huge container filled with words—words that are waiting to be loosed and expressed through the prophetic ministry in music.

The Father's heart desires to pour out His divine frequencies through the musicians. Music and songs are keys that unlock the heavenly portals for certain prophetic words. When a song is played in any key, the notes become a chord—a harmonizing frequency—that triggers the opening through which prophetic words will flow and find their mark.

The key for that particular moment in time is given by the Spirit of God. It could be the key of C, the key of G, or any key! But it's the musicians who hear that key from the Father.

God has words that He wants to be released on the earth that have never been expressed before. Our vocabulary has looked like a first-grade reading book compared to what God wants to say. He wants to express Himself through the musicians, through the prophets, and through the spirit of prophecy operating in the body of Christ.

I have often thought of these principles of sound, music, and frequency. There can be no question that music is powerful in every generation, in every plane of existence, Christian or not.

But music anointed with the life frequency of God is the most powerful. Music from the Spirit of God brings harmony, unity, and healing.

> **Music anointed with the life frequency of God is the most powerful.**

Musicians in the body of Christ, above all, should be able to recognize that their calling is to pave the way for unity and harmony in a service so that whoever is ministering can flow into that anointing.

There is a frequency of discord when things are "out of divine order." When someone is "off-key" in singing, everyone knows it. When a musician or worship leader is "off-key" in the spirit, it is very noticeable. What do I mean by that?

I have been in meetings where the worship leader or musicians were in competition with the pastor or leader of that meeting. No part of ministry is a competitive sport!

If we put aside our desire for recognition and expression of self and instead seek the unity of the Spirit, we will experience ever more powerful manifestations of God.

We must press into those spiritual places where the expression of God exists and unlock them so the spirit of prophecy can flow. We do this by allowing the Holy Spirit to do what He wants and relinquishing our pre-formed ideas taught by religious traditions and self-interests.

The Anointing Activates Prophetic Words

The prophet's ministry in this hour is vital because it's the prophet who creates the vision and hope that is set before us. God uses a prophet to speak forth His vision on the earth.

First Samuel 3:19 says that Samuel grew in the knowledge of the Lord, and none of his words failed. Prophetic words have to be spoken for them to come to pass.

The anointing of the Spirit upon the spoken word activates and releases seed into the seen realm. The process starts in the unseen realm—the realm of the spirit—and cannot affect the physical realm until it is spoken.

> Sometimes even today, prophetic words are shrouded in mystery.

When men of old prophesied about the coming Messiah, their message was given in words. The Spirit came upon those words, but they were shrouded in mystery. The devil had no idea what was about to happen. Jesus, however, perfectly fulfilled every prophecy.

Sometimes even today, prophetic words are shrouded in mystery. But after the prophecy happens, we are amazed and declare, "So that's what that meant!" It's not so important that what the prophet says is fully understood, but simply that the *seed* of those words is released onto the earth.

Our understanding (or lack thereof) will neither cause nor prevent a prophetic word from happening. Think about it. How many people over the centuries truly understood the Messianic prophecies and how they would come to pass?

Prophetic Dream—Fire

In November 2003, I had a long, detailed, and disturbing dream. Large trucks with flashing lights were parked at the front gate of our 40-acre farm in the dream. Many other trucks and vehicles with flashing lights lined the road that goes to our property.

Out of a window in my house, I saw people open our gates. Others were driving across our yard. I told my husband to get out there quickly as I put on a protective jumpsuit before running out the door.

All of our pets were in animal carriers and loaded in the back of my SUV (which I didn't own at that time). I was concerned about the pets because they had been in the SUV for a long time.

As the large vehicles with lights drove across the yard, they ran over and broke sewer pipes, tore up our fences, and made large ruts in the ground from their weight. People were everywhere. Bulldozers were tearing up the fields and cutting roads into our property.

Throughout the dream, my husband and I kept getting separated for some reason. I tried calling him on his cellphone, but he never heard it ring because of the noise. Eventually, I found him in the hayfield helping the people who were on our property.

I was very upset in the dream and kept racing all over the property trying to stop what was happening. I woke up feeling frustrated and exhausted.

Reality

Two years later, almost to the day I had that dream, wildfires broke out in Oklahoma. On the first day of the fires, wind gusts were up to 70 miles per hour. I spent most of the afternoon securing loose objects and checking for wind damage to our property.

Around 4:30 p.m., my husband and I went outside to feed our farm animals. We saw thick, black smoke to the southwest and realized that the fire was racing directly toward us.

I immediately called my mother and asked her and my dad to pray. Then I called 911.

For two hours, we did our best to secure the property. We watered the yard with hoses and sprayed the roofs of our outbuildings. The small animals were put in crates and loaded in my SUV. I moved the vehicle as far away from the fire as possible. Then my husband and I began to cut the fences so the cattle and horses could run free.

The firefighters couldn't control the fire, which was started when an electrical line touched the roof of a metal building. Fueled by high winds and tall grass, the fire jumped the road to the west, and a 20-foot wall of fire a half-mile wide roared across our hayfield.

Fire trucks from several counties gathered in our yard to protect our house and barns while bulldozers cut a firebreak to stop the fire's progression. Our front yard was filled with emergency vehicles with lights flashing, law enforcement officers, volunteers with shovels and wet blankets, 4-wheelers, and assorted trucks. Even a local news station set up a satellite dish to cover what was happening.

The firemen and volunteers fought the fire for the next eight hours. We lease 200 acres of land, and the fire burned all but a few acres of it. The five acres where our house, barn, and outbuildings are located weren't touched. The fire stopped at our north, west, and east property lines.

We fought the fires all night long. At 4 a.m. the following day, I was frustrated and exhausted but overwhelmingly grateful. When I looked out the window, fire trucks were still parked on the road near our house, standing guard and watching for any flare-ups. At that instant, I remembered what I had dreamed two years before.

Even though I never saw a fire in the dream, I believe things were imparted to my spirit that caused me to make the right decisions when I didn't know what was about to happen.

For one thing, I kept feeling that the field near the house needed to be cut. Two weeks before the fire, my husband took the tractor and brush hog and cut a swath around the field that left a 30-foot firebreak close to our home.

Right before the fire, I also felt "led" to buy a 4-wheel drive all-terrain vehicle with a dump bed that seats three people. And just as I had dreamed, I ended up transporting volunteer firefighters with their equipment around the property.

Everything that was in the dream happened in startling detail. I literally saw *everything* that happened that night in a prophetic dream with *no* understanding of what it really meant. However, I ended up with exactly what I needed, including the SUV, the ATV, and a fire break around our property.

I sometimes wonder if I had been given the full revelation of the meaning of that dream, if it would have helped me, or would it have caused me to fear. But God gave me enough clues to prepare me for what was about to happen.

That dream shed new light on the importance of paying attention to every aspect of life that might contain guidance, including dreams.

CHAPTER 7

SIGNS AND WONDERS AND THE WORKING OF MIRACLES

In the Old Testament, we see various types of prophets. One was a preacher of righteousness who warned and exhorted people against wickedness. Jonah fits into this category.

God sent Jonah to Nineveh to cry out against the wickedness of the people. When he finally obeyed, Jonah delivered the word of the Lord that Nineveh would be overthrown in 40 days.

We know, of course, that the people repented, and God spared them, which made Jonah very angry. After what he had prophesied and been through, was he now a false prophet because his prophecy did not come to pass?

This is an example of a conditional prophecy. Basically, it states what will happen if you continue doing what you are doing. The Ninevites repented and changed their ways. God is merciful, so Jonah's prophecy resulted in their salvation instead of their destruction.

> Was he now a false prophet because his prophecy did not come to pass?

Jeremiah, the weeping prophet, is also an example of a preacher of righteousness who blazed up in anger and declared the sins of the people. When you study his ministry, you see that he operated in pulling down strongholds. *"See, I have this day appointed you to the oversight of the nations and of the kingdoms to root out and pull down, to destroy and to overthrow, to build and to plant"* (Jer. 1:10 AMPC).

Jeremiah was told to root out, pull down strongholds, and throw down kingdoms—kingdoms of the devil, the prince of the power of the air, and rulers of demonic strongholds.

He was also told to *"build and to plant."* After removing the evil, something had to be put in its place. There is a seed sowing of righteousness through the prophet's mouth that builds a reign of righteousness in places where wickedness has previously ruled.

Seers

Another type of prophet is a seer. This prophet looked into the spirit realm and saw what God showed him. He had visions and supernatural revelations. Daniel and Ezekiel were two such men. God revealed to them what would happen in the end times. These future prophetic words contained the gift of the word of wisdom.

The prophet Samuel was a seer who also operated in the area of words. *"The Lord was with him and let none of his words fall to the ground"* (1 Sam. 3:19 ESV). He was a spokesman for God, or you could say he was the "mouth" of God. In his day, people were still attuned to God and would listen to words.

In Jesus' time, that was not so. The scribes and Pharisees weren't interested in what Jesus had to say. They asked for signs. But Jesus said, *"A wicked and adulterous generation demands a sign, but none will be given it except the sign of the prophet Jonah"* (Matt. 12:39). What was the sign Jesus referred to? Jonah's preaching and exhortation.

Jesus told the scribes and Pharisees He wouldn't give them any sign. They were the religious people of their day and had no business asking for one. Signs and wonders were for the unbeliever and those who did not know the true God, the God of Israel.

Supernatural Signs

As the generations following Jonah became more wicked, God anointed Elijah and Elisha to perform signs and wonders. In one incident, Elijah gathered together 450 prophets of Baal at Mount Carmel. The prophets of Baal and Elijah both prepared bulls to sacrifice. Elijah told the false prophets to call on Baal to consume their sacrifice with fire. They petitioned Baal for hours, and nothing happened.

Elijah made it hard for himself. He dug a trench around his offering and poured four jars of water on the bull and the wood, filling the trench with water. When Elijah called on the Name of the Lord, fire shot down from heaven and consumed the sacrifice.

Signs and wonders were manifested in miracle after miracle in Elisha and Elijah's ministry because of the perverseness of their generation.

Prophet of Judgement

Also involved in the prophet's ministry is judgment. In First Kings 13, a prophet came to town and went to the altar of the Lord as Jeroboam, King of Israel, was about to make an offering. The man of God prophesied to the altar.

> *"O altar, O altar, this is what the Lord says: 'A son named Josiah will be born to the house of David, and upon you he will sacrifice the priests of the high places who burn incense upon you, and human bones will be burned upon you.'" That day the man of God gave a sign, saying, "The Lord has spoken this sign: 'Surely the altar will be split apart, and the ashes upon it will be poured out.'"*

1 Kings 13:2-3

The king became angry when he heard what the prophet said and wanted to kill the man of God. When Jeroboam stretched out his hand and said, "Seize him," his hand withered up. That is a demonstration of God's judgment.

One time as Elisha was going to Bethel, a group of young men began mocking him, calling him "baldhead." Elisha called down a curse on them, and two bears came out of the woods and mauled 42 of them.

A time will come in our day when true prophets of God will be raised up and begin to operate in the same realm the Old Testament prophets did, including judgment.

Counterfeit Miracles

What's happening on the earth right now—in this day, this time, and this hour—is that the world system is building up for that horrendous period called the Great Tribulation. During the Tribulation—and even some time before it starts—increased angelic activity will take place in ways we've never even heard of. And the earth will experience signs and wonders that people today have never seen.

The beast—the antichrist that will come forth—will manifest a counterfeit gift of the working of miracles because that is the only way people will believe. Words will have lost their power. Nobody will believe anything but signs and wonders.

But before the antichrist can operate in counterfeit gifts, a true manifestation of the Spirit of God must happen. So get ready. Two gifts that will come into prominence are the working of miracles and the gift of faith. We will see great manifestations of the working of miracles and supernatural deliverance by angels through the gift of faith long before the antichrist comes on the scene.

During the Tribulation, God will raise up two prophets who will operate in the gift of working of miracles. They will call fire down from heaven and cause droughts to come. They will stand on the streets of Jerusalem and prophesy by the Spirit of the true God. And for a time, they will be supernaturally protected by the gift of faith.

We are leading up to that time right now.

Signs for Our Nation

At one time, the United States of America stood on principles based on God's Word. For many years, this nation has been sensitive to the Spirit of God, but it has become more perverse. We have reached a point where God is going to start showing signs and wonders.

When people are sensitive to the Holy Spirit and follow righteousness, we don't see much of a display of God's power in judgment. But as a nation becomes more wicked, we will start seeing a buildup of the power of God in an Elijah-like fashion.

The prophet's ministry has been coming into prominence in our day. And God will move in the gift of the working of miracles to control the elements and nature and in magnificent manifestations.

Joel promised it: *"And I will show signs and wonders in the heavens, and on the earth, blood and fire and columns of smoke"* (Joel 2:30 AMPC). Peter reiterated that in Acts 2:19.

Kings, Prophets, and the Nations

The day is here when kings of the earth and presidents of nations will call upon the prophets. They will say, "Bring me a prophet who can show me how to direct this country." It may not become public knowledge, but it will happen just as King Jehoshaphat said, *"Is there no prophet of the Lord here by whom we may inquire of the Lord?"* (2 Kings 3:11 AMPC). And like the prophets of old, today's prophets will have a precise word from God for the leader.

> **We will start seeing a buildup of the power of God in an Elijah-like fashion.**

The following prophecy was given on May 27, 1977, by my father, Charles Capps.

> But I say unto you, I will reveal Myself in a manner in those days that men have not known. The nations of the world will stand in awe at that which shall come forth from Me.
>
> They will find themselves in dire need. They will come up against problems for which there is no answer in the world system.
>
> But from this nation, there shall go forth men anointed as prophets of God, and My Spirit shall dwell in the midst of them. These men shall be called forth by the nations of the world, saying, "Send us a prophet of God that he may reveal

unto us the ways of God for the things that have worked in the days past will not work now. And we have seen and know that it works in that land!"

CHAPTER 8

THE ANOINTING IS TRANSFERABLE

The anointing that operates upon a prophet is transmittable, although the office is not. The office of a prophet is a divine calling by God. A person cannot legitimately choose to be a prophet or an apostle or any ministry gift. It is by the ordination of God alone.

But sitting under someone's ministry will allow their anointing to spill over on you while you are in the presence of that anointing. You may prophesy or have other manifestations of the Spirit through you.

However, that anointing will only come upon you and abide if you first develop a godly character, submit yourself to God, and become skillful in the Word. Obedience to God is paramount as a minister is simply a vessel of the Spirit of God.

Even though the Spirit came upon Saul and he prophesied, the anointing departed from him. *"But*

> The office of a prophet is a divine calling by God.

the Spirit of the Lord departed from Saul" (1 Sam. 16:14 KJV). It did not abide in him because of his disobedience and willfulness.

God once used a donkey, but the Spirit did not abide in or upon that donkey all its life. The gifts of the Spirit do not prove the vessel has a good moral character. It only proves that God desires to manifest Himself to all humanity.

In First Samuel 19, not only did Saul prophesy when he came in contact with a company of prophets, but so did the men he sent to capture David.

> *Word came to Saul: "David is in Naioth at Ramah";*
> *so he sent men to capture him. But when they saw*
> *a group of prophets prophesying, with Samuel*
> *standing there as their leader, the Spirit of God*
> *came on Saul's men, and they also prophesied.*
> *Saul was told about it, and he sent more men, and*
> *they prophesied too. Saul sent men a third time,*
> *and they also prophesied. Finally, he himself left*
> *for Ramah and went to the great cistern at Seku.*
> *And he asked, "Where are Samuel and David?"*
>
> *"Over in Naioth at Ramah," they said. So Saul*
> *went to Naioth at Ramah. But the Spirit of God*
> *came even on him, and he walked along prophe-*
> *sying until he came to Naioth.*
>
> **1 Samuel 19:19-23 NIV**

We see that the Spirit of God can come upon people who are not called to the office of the prophet and cause them to prophesy under the influence of that anointing.

A Double Portion

Elisha was a disciple of the prophet Elijah and served him until Elijah was caught up to heaven. He received a double portion of Elijah's anointing.

Elisha was also called to the office of prophet—which was evident by the works he did—and he lived upright and obedient to God. Therefore, the anointing came on him to abide and function in that office just as it had on Elijah, except it doubled.

When they had crossed, Elijah said to Elisha, "Ask what I shall do for you, before I am taken from you." And Elisha said, "Please let there be a double portion of your spirit on me." And he said, "You have asked a hard thing; yet, if you see me as I am being taken from you, it shall be so for you, but if you do not see me, it shall not be so." And as they still went on and talked, behold, chariots of fire and horses of fire separated the two of them. And Elijah went up by a whirlwind into heaven. And Elisha saw it and he cried, "My father, my father! The chariots of Israel and its horsemen!" And he saw him no more.

Then he took hold of his own clothes and tore them in two pieces. And he took up the cloak of Elijah that had fallen from him and went back and stood on the bank of the Jordan. Then he took the cloak of Elijah that had fallen from him and struck the water, saying, "Where is the Lord, the God of Elijah?" And when he had struck the water, the water was parted to the one side and to the other, and Elisha went over.

Now when the sons of the prophets who were at Jericho saw him opposite them, they said, "The spirit of Elijah rests on Elisha." And they came to meet him and bowed to the ground before him.

2 Kings 2:9-15 ESV

Wrong Motives

You don't get a double portion of an anointing just because you're around a ministry. The anointing doesn't fall on you and abide because you had a close encounter with a prophetic anointing or the gifts of healing. You have to go after it, your heart and motives must be right, and you must carefully listen to and obey the Word of God and His directions.

Gehazi was Elisha's servant and followed Elisha the way Elisha followed Elijah. However, Gehazi didn't receive any anointing because his heart was not right.

Second Kings 5 tells how Naaman, a commander in the Syrian army, was healed of leprosy. Naaman was so grateful for being healed that he wanted to bless Elisha with a gift, but

Elisha wouldn't accept it. Gehazi, on the other hand, felt that he could benefit from Naaman's gratitude.

So after Naaman left, Gehazi ran after him. When he caught up to Naaman, he made up a story about two young prophets and Elisha needing help after all. Naaman gladly gave Gehazi money and clothing.

When Gehazi returned, Elisha questioned his whereabouts. Gehazi lied about what he just did and was struck with leprosy. (See 2 Kings 5:1-27.)

The fact that Gehazi lied tells us what we need to know about his moral character. Even though he was constantly around the anointing, his heart was not open to the spiritual laws that governed the Kingdom of God.

Like Saul, he was not open to correction but was unrepentant. Both Saul and Gehazi had opportunities to admit their moral failures and disobedience. But both of them chose to lie and hide the wickedness and rebellion in their hearts.

Rewards for Ministering to a Prophet

Scripture also shows us how being a blessing to a prophet brings rewards. The Shunammite woman received great rewards for ministering to Elisha. When

> Both Saul and Gehazi had opportunities to admit their moral failures and disobedience.

the prophet first went to the village of Shunem, this woman invited him to dinner. As time passed, he always stopped at her home when he was traveling through. Eventually, the Shunammite woman's husband built a room for Elisha to stay in when he was in the area.

In return for her kindness, Elisha prophesied to the Shunammite woman, and she conceived and gave birth to a son. When her son was older, he became ill and died. But the boy was resurrected when Elisha prayed for him.

Later, Elisha warned the woman of a famine that would last for seven years. She and her household traveled to the land of the Philistines and stayed there for the duration of the famine.

After the famine ended, the Shunammite woman returned to Israel and appealed to the king so her land and home would be restored to her. At the exact moment she came before the king, Gehazi was telling him how Elisha had raised her son from the dead. The king restored her land and all its produce from the time she left to when she stood before the king.

You can see how blessing Elisha yielded great rewards for the Shunammite woman.

Don't Get Infected with a Wrong Spirit

The anointing on a person can be a desirable thing, but you must be careful whom you associate with. When you sit under a ministry, you may pick up the good points. But if you are not wise and discerning, you can also pick up the bad points—weaknesses, attitudes, impatience, and ideas that don't agree with scripture.

Take what is good and be discerning. Even highly anointed ministers are subject to attitudes and imperfections like everyone else.

Follow the leading in your spirit and obey that inward witness.

It doesn't matter who told you about a minister or who approves of a ministry. Follow the leading in your spirit and obey that inward witness.

Never allow someone to lay hands on you unless you have a witness in your spirit that it's right. If you have the slightest question or if what seems to be happening in the spirit makes you feel a little strange, keep your distance from it and seek the guidance of the Holy Spirit.

Be sure the Spirit of God is in operation when you are at a service, and be aware of any attitudes that are not godly. False spirits can operate so close to the real thing that you won't recognize that what is happening is not of God unless you listen to your spirit.

When the real Spirit of God is in a service, peace is ministered, and it feels so right. It feels righter than any right you have ever felt.

When a false spirit is operating, there's no doubt that something supernatural is going on. But instead of peace, you have a strange feeling, and that's not the Spirit of God.

CHAPTER 9

ALL BELIEVERS CAN PROPHESY

Many years ago as I was ministering in Westville, Oklahoma, I began to prophesy and heard myself say, "There's more to prophecy and prophesying than you thought." I didn't know what that might be, so I had to keep talking to find out what God was saying.

The Spirit of God continued, "Don't say, 'I can't prophesy,' for you can. You can prophesy in your prayer closet. You can prophesy in your car. And you can prophesy when you're alone. Did I not say that in the last days, I would pour out my Spirit upon all flesh, and your sons and daughters shall prophesy?"

Every born-again Christian must come to the realization that they can stand in their prayer place and prophesy. The Spirit of God went on to say that He would raise up the entire body of Christ to prophesy because of what He wants brought to pass on the earth. Christians will call God's desires into existence and create them by prophesying.

One thing the Spirit told us to do during that meeting was to stand in our prayer closet, raise our hands, and say, "Thus saith the Lord God Almighty, the Word of the Lord will go behind the

Iron Curtain. It shall not be stopped. My Word shall be fulfilled in every part of the earth. And My Spirit shall move behind the Iron Curtain. There shall be a great revival there among My people, for I shall move, and no one shall stop Me."

This meeting was in 1978. The world saw the dissolution of the U.S.S.R. in the early '90s, and men and women of God have testified to the move of the Spirit among the people there.

The Spirit told us to prophesy to our government and say, "Thus saith the Lord God, the United States of America shall not go under. It shall stand as a righteous nation. I am moving in the United States, and I shall root out the wickedness of this government, and I shall move the righteous in."

(I believe if we as the body of Christ had applied what we were told, this nation would be in a very different place today than where we are now.)

> If we as the body of Christ had applied what we were told, this nation would be in a very different place today than where we are now.

Prophesy to a City

Years ago, I was in Salt Lake City, Utah. Late one night, I was in a hotel room standing on the balcony looking out at the city's skyline when I heard the Spirit of God say, "Prophesy to this city."

At first I thought, "How am I supposed to do that?" I wondered if I should hold a meeting at the civic center and prophesy. Or maybe I needed to get a sound system and set it up on the balcony. "What am I supposed to do?"

The Lord said, "Prophesy right here."

I knew the effect of prophecy did not depend on someone hearing it because Jesus said, *"The words that I speak to you are spirit and they are life"* (John 6:63). They're alive. They're active. They're energizing. They're effective. They're operative. And they affect things, people, and places without anybody ever hearing the prophecy.

So I stood on the balcony, raised my hands, and said, "Salt Lake City, hear the Word of your God. I declare in the Name of Jesus and by His Word that revival is in this city. I rebuke that which has come against the body of Christ, and I speak unity. For thus saith the Lord, 'My Body shall come together in this city, and there shall be a great revival.'"

About six months later, I ran into a friend as he was leaving town and asked where he was going.

"Salt Lake City," he replied.

"What's going on there?"

"Well," he said, "there's been a lot of division in that city. But the entire body of Christ has come together. I'm speaking at the civic center, and all the churches there are supporting the meeting. A great revival is going on!"

God's Word will never return to Him void or without any results (see Isa. 55:11). God needs our obedience to speak out prophetic words so He can move in situations and change things, including the spiritual atmosphere of cities, states, and nations. His anointing on our words produces the same results. It will accomplish the will of God on the earth.

Yes, *You* Can Prophesy

Never say, "I can't. I can't preach. I can't prophesy. I can't do any of these things." Yes, you can. You absolutely can.

God is raising up the prophet's ministry in this hour. As a prophet prophesies, the anointing will also come on you if you allow it. You can go home and prophesy the same thing in the privacy of your home. The more people say it, the more we will come into unity. And in the unity of faith, we will see God's will come to pass.

In Numbers 11, Moses was burdened down with the complaints of the people and cried out to God. *"I am not able to carry all these people alone, because the burden is too heavy for me"* (Num. 11:14 AMPC). God said to Moses:

> *Gather for Me seventy men of the elders of Israel whom you know to be the elders of the people and officers over them; and bring them to the Tent of Meeting and let them stand there with you.*
>
> *And I will come down and talk with you there; and I will take of the Spirit which is upon you and will put It upon them; and they shall bear the burden of the people with you, so that you may not have to bear it yourself alone.*
>
> **Numbers 11:16-17 AMPC**

God took the anointing that was on Moses and put it on 70 elders. That way, Moses wouldn't have to carry the burden by himself. When the anointing was placed on the elders, *"they prophesied [sounding forth the praises of God and declaring His will]"* (Num. 11:25 AMPC).

One of the reasons God wants you to prophesy is to declare His will on the earth. He wants you to say, "Thus saith the Lord God, the will of God is done on earth as it is in heaven. The will of God is done in my life on earth as it is in heaven. The will of God is done in this city as it is in heaven. I speak the will of God."

One of the reasons God wants you to prophesy is to declare His will on the earth.

In Numbers 11, two of the elders did not go to the Tent of Meeting.

> *But there remained two men in the camp named Eldad and Medad. The Spirit rested upon them, and they were of those who were selected and listed, yet they did not go out to the Tent [as told to do], but they prophesied in the camp.*
>
> *And a young man ran to Moses and said, Eldad and Medad are prophesying [sounding forth the praises of God and declaring His will] in the camp.*

Joshua son of Nun, the minister of Moses, one of his chosen men, said, My lord Moses, forbid them!

But Moses said to him, Are you envious or jealous for my sake? Would that all the Lord's people were prophets and that the Lord would put His Spirit upon them!

Numbers 11:26-29 AMPC

God has put His Spirit upon His sons and daughters to prophesy today. They will prophesy to cities and to people— not to the person's face but in the privacy of their home in their place of prayer. They will say, "So-and-so, hear the Word of the Lord. You are a disciple taught of the Lord, and you will become obedient to His will in Jesus' name. Your eyes are opened by His Holy Spirit."

> **Christians will be called upon to prophesy to the government.**

And because they prophesied, the Word will be quickened to that individual.

Christians will be called upon to prophesy to the government. They will command it to become a righteous government.

In the Old Testament, there were a few prophets who prophesied here and there. Today, God is putting His Spirit upon the body of Christ to prophesy. As the anointing comes on believers, they will prophesy in unison with one sound. And the sound of their prophecies—the declaration of the Word—will be heard throughout the earth.

Tell These Bones to Live!

If you think prophesying to a city or nation is strange, Ezekiel was told to prophesy to dead, dry bones!

Ezekiel was carried away by the Spirit of God to a valley filled with dry bones. God asked him, *"Can these bones live?"* (Ezek. 37:3). Then God told Ezekiel to prophesy to the bones. He said:

> *"O dry bones, hear the word of the Lord. Thus says the Lord God to these bones: Behold, I will cause breath to enter you, and you shall live. And I will lay sinews upon you, and will cause flesh to come upon you, and cover you with skin, and put breath in you, and you shall live, and you shall know that I am the Lord."*
>
> *So I prophesied as I was commanded. And as I prophesied, there was a sound, and behold, a rattling, and the bones came together, bone to its bone. And I looked, and behold, there were sinews on them, and flesh had come upon them, and skin had covered them. But there was no breath in them. Then he said to me, "Prophesy to the breath; prophesy, son of man, and say to the breath, Thus says the Lord God: Come from the four winds, O*

*breath, and breathe on these slain, that they may
live." So I prophesied as he commanded me, and
the breath came into them, and they lived and
stood on their feet, an exceedingly great army.*

Ezekiel 37:4-10 ESV

Notice that the bones arranged themselves in order. Divine order is coming. The breath of the Spirit of Life is bringing the structure of the Church into divine alignment so that Christ's Body becomes strong and puts His enemies underfoot. That which has seemed dead will come to life.

Are there areas in your life that are dried up and dead? You can prophesy life to them! God is a God of resurrection and restoration.

Shake Satan's Kingdom

When you prophesy the Word of the Lord, a great trembling—a shaking and rattling—happens in satan's kingdom. When you shake and rattle the devil, he begins to fall and move aside because Jesus gave the Church authority over all the power of the enemy.

I have said under the spirit of prophecy, "Thus saith the Lord, you foul spirit that has ruled over the midwestern states, over Nevada. I speak to you, you foul spirit. You are defeated, and you come down from your high place."

When the Lord anoints you to speak, His Word shakes satan's kingdom beyond repair. When a member of the body of

Christ stands up and boldly declares God's Word in the face of the devil, in the face of defeat, in the face of sin, sickness, and death, opposition must move aside. The gates of hell will not prevail against the Name of Jesus, and hell cannot stop the advancement of a believer with the Word in his mouth.

> **Hell cannot stop the advancement of a believer with the Word in his mouth.**

The spirit of prophecy will come upon you and anoint your words and cause you to intercede with the spirit of prophecy, and cause you to pray with the spirit of prophecy, and cause you to declare God's Word by the spirit of prophecy.

Every believer can speak the Lord's words under His anointing by His power. That anointing will come upon you and rest on you, and you will prophesy, for God is pouring out His spirit upon all flesh. And as flesh and blood, you qualify!

Called to Help

The adversary, the devil, is about to get his kingdom shaken even more. God took the spirit that was on Moses and placed it upon others to help him.

In the Old Testament, we read about the anointing that rested upon the prophet, the priest, and the king. However, in *this* day, the anointing abides *in* each of us. First John 2:27

says that "the anointing you receive abides in you" because of the New Birth.

You may not be "called" to the office of the fivefold ministry, but you may be called to step under the anointing of another in support and help.

When everyone in the body finds their proper function and finds the grace and anointing to flow in the Spirit, we will see the measure of the stature of the fullness of Christ (see Eph. 4:13). We are His temple and dwelling place.

When the Tent of Meeting was about to be built in the wilderness, God raised up skilled men to complete the task.

> *The Lord said to Moses, "See, I have called by name Bezalel the son of Uri, son of Hur, of the tribe of Judah, and I have filled him with the Spirit of God, with ability and intelligence, with knowledge and all craftsmanship, to devise artistic designs, to work in gold, silver, and bronze, in cutting stones for setting, and in carving wood, to work in every craft. And behold, I have appointed with him Oholiab, the son of Ahisamach, of the tribe of Dan. And I have given to all able men ability, that they may make all that I have commanded you."*
>
> **Exodus 31:1-6 ESV**

God raises up skilled and anointed people to help bring God's plan to fruition. They are called to *assist* those appointed to the fivefold ministry and will reap the rewards of that "prophet." Those in the ministry of helps can flow in the gifts of the Spirit to support the anointing upon the ministers or the mission of the organization.

God has poured out his Spirit on *all* flesh. Everyone has their part in this end-time revival. People in the helps ministry can receive the anointing to function where they are called, be keen in the spirit, and help in supernatural ways. The gifts of the Spirit will work in the helps ministry just as they do in the fivefold ministry gifts.

The building of the Temple, or Tent of Meeting, required organization, structure, and teamwork. It also needed a vision or blueprint of the final results. Without the direction of a leader or overseer, the goal could not be reached.

Every person and every task is essential to reach its completion. As each member of the body of Christ is filled with the Spirit of God to flow in *their* ability and talents, the body of Christ will grow up to God's original design.

CHAPTER 10

GOVERNED BY THE SPIRIT

Pastors can be uncomfortable giving freedom to members of the congregation or a guest preacher to minister by the Spirit. That is understandable since abuse and misunderstanding about the governing of the gifts of the Spirit have happened, resulting in confusion and occasionally a tug of war over who is in charge of the service.

Hopefully, the Holy Spirit is! But God is a God of order, and the Holy Spirit works within the authority structure of the church or meeting.

Most significantly, the spoken gifts of tongues, interpretation, and prophecy have been curtailed because those who spoke out did not understand this structure and order of the Spirit. We can complain and make excuses, but these abuses (or interruptions) could have been handled simply by teaching the etiquette of the Spirit.

What causes questions and concerns for people is seeing and experiencing the anointing of God upon someone or a great moving of the Spirit that slips out of divine order. The Holy Spirit does not interrupt Himself. When one of the fivefold ministries is speaking, prophesying, or laying hands on people, the Holy Spirit will not move upon another person to *interrupt* what is happening.

As agents of free will, we can recognize that the Holy Spirit does not take over or force you to do anything. He is a gentleman and leads without force. Whatever you receive from God is under your control. You can speak out a prophecy or hold your peace. Whether or not you give a word depends on the order of the meeting. Paul tells us in First Corinthians 14:32-33 (AMP):

> *For the spirits of prophets are subject to the prophets [the prophecy is under the speaker's control, and he can stop speaking]; for God [who is the source of their prophesying] is not a God of confusion and disorder but of peace and order.*

Whatever you receive from God is under your control.

Granted, Paul did not really need to tell us this because it is not good manners to interrupt another person speaking in private or public. However, the situation can be understood by the following example.

Learning the Rules of the Road

When I learned how to drive a car, I did not know all the principles and rules that governed traffic. Actually, I learned to drive on the farm—first on a tractor and then in an old car that I drove on farm roads.

It was fun! It was new! It was exhilarating! No longer was I limited to walking or riding my bicycle. The excitement was a real thrill for a 13-year-old.

The first thing I wanted to experience was speed! How fast could I go? How sharp could I turn? Then I wanted to demonstrate my talent by showing off to friends. That meant *more speed* and more maneuvers to show how good I really was at driving. (In case you need to be reminded, this kind of thinking is why insurance rates for teenage drivers are so high.)

As I ventured out onto the main road, I discovered other drivers were out there too. Since I did not know what they were thinking and where they were going, I needed to learn what the regulations were when other people were on the road.

I knew that policemen would direct traffic and tell you what to do. But I lived way out in the country, and the nearest town, England, Arkansas, had fewer than 3,000 people. There were no traffic policemen.

Then there was the question of four-way stop signs. Who goes first? Do you get out of your car and draw straws?

Are you seeing the point?

Who's in Charge?

Ultimately, the Holy Spirit should be the one in charge of a church service. But He has authorized the pastor or whoever is in charge of the service to direct the traffic. In the same way we can go to a driver's education class, receive a book, and study the regulations to learn how to safely navigate through traffic, we can be taught by the fivefold ministry gifts on how to navigate and flow in the gifts of the Spirit safely and in order.

Pastors are not the only ones uncomfortable with the public manifestation of the gifts of the Spirit. Even believers in the church or outside meetings seem to be uncomfortable. There is a feeling that someone may speak out of turn, speak something that isn't right, or try to take over the service. If believers are uncomfortable, what do you think someone who does not know about the gifts would feel like if there was a sudden outburst in tongues?

> We can be taught by the fivefold ministry gifts on how to navigate and flow in the gifts of the Spirit safely and in order.

God forbid that we lose the manifestations of the Spirit because we are afraid! If we desire and covet the gifts to be in the church, surely God has the answer for how this can be done to bless everyone.

Is it possible to have powerful manifestations of the Spirit and also correction by the Spirit?

Paul gives us basic principles in First Corinthians 14 that govern the flow of the gifts of the Spirit within a church or a meeting of believers.

1. It must be done decently and in order.

2. Speak one at a time.

3. The gift must magnify Jesus as Lord.

4. The gift will edify and build up the body of Christ.

5. The word of prophecy must be judged.

6. Despise not prophesying.

7. Don't quench the Spirit.

Paul gave these principles to govern the manifestations of the gifts of the Spirit. Each pastor of a church has the freedom to regulate the "traffic," so to speak. For instance, a pastor may instruct the people that they will ask from the pulpit, "Does someone in the congregation have a word of prophecy or tongues and interpretation?"

If a believer whom God uses in prophecy is present, the minister may give them permission to either give a signal or come to the platform if they have a word for the congregation.

Most of the time, the pastor recognizes the anointing and flow of the Spirit. This is great, but it also can present a problem when the pastor doesn't understand the etiquette of the Spirit in flowing with other ministers in the fivefold ministry.

A common scenario that my dad and I encountered many times was being invited to a church and having the pastor get up and preach our sermon before they invited us to the pulpit. Sometimes a word or two from the leader confirms the message you are about to give, which fits and is a blessing.

But many times, the minister would get under the anointing that was on my dad. They got excited and taught or preached most of the points in Dad's message. Nothing was wrong with what was said, but the pastor invited a guest to *feed* the people. But he served the *whole meal* before the guest got behind the pulpit.

Unless you have been in this position, it's hard to imagine what it's like to follow that. It's like trying to serve a delicious meal when everyone has already eaten. You have to work to keep the people awake and get them hungry again!

The anointing is exciting. There's nothing like receiving the meat of the Word delivered by the Spirit to a hungry soul. But people benefit the most when they have time to digest and assimilate what they have received.

Love Governs

In any setting, always let love guide you. If you are in the cloud of God's glory in a meeting and time is suspended, you could be standing for hours and wonder how time passed. If you are not in the glory, your feet may hurt, and you could be tired and hungry. Even Jesus and His disciples were concerned about the multitudes far from food and home.

When we come together as a body of believers, courtesy is always appreciated.

CHAPTER 11

PROPHESYING AS PART OF THE WHOLE

First Corinthians 13 is often called the love chapter. It is sandwiched between chapter 12, which teaches on the gifts and callings of the Spirit, and chapter 14, which emphasizes the etiquette of the spoken gifts. I always looked at First Corinthians 13 as a pause to remind the Corinthians that everything is done in love.

However, Paul did not write in chapter and verse. This chapter ties into recognizing the whole body of Christ. It takes *every* part of *every* ministry gift to give us an accurate picture of the realm of the Spirit.

> *Love never ends. As for prophecies, they will pass away; as for tongues, they will cease; as for knowledge, it will pass away. For we know in part and we prophesy in part, but when the perfect comes, the partial will pass away. When I was a child, I spoke like a child, I thought like a child, I reasoned like a child. When I became a man, I gave*

up childish ways. For now we see in a mirror dimly, but then face to face. Now I know in part; then I shall know fully, even as I have been fully known.

First Corinthians 13:8-12 ESV

Consider what Paul says in chapter 12 about the different parts of the body and what they contribute to the whole. When you look at the anointings of the apostles, prophets, evangelists, pastors, and teachers, you will see that no one has everything.

No one prophet has the complete picture. Each prophet prophesies in part—the part that God showed them. That is why some prophecies seem to be contradictory. When more than one person is prophesying about the same thing, each person is given one piece of a puzzle. Until all the prophecies come together, no one has a full revelation or understanding.

> No one prophet has the complete picture.

Look at the prophecies concerning the Messiah and decide which one was correct. God told Micah that the Messiah would come out of Bethlehem.

But you, O Bethlehem Ephrathah, who are too little to be among the clans of Judah, from you shall come forth for me one who is to be ruler in Israel,

— 124 —

whose coming forth is from of old, from ancient days.

Micah 5:2 ESV

Hosea prophesied that the Messiah would come out of Egypt.

When Israel was a child, I loved him, and out of Egypt I called my son.

Hosea 11:1 ESV

But the prophet Isaiah said the light of the Messiah would shine in Zebulun and Naphtali (see Isa. 9:1-7). Which prophet was the true prophet? They all said seemingly different things.

Looking back, we can see that Jesus fulfilled each one of these contradictory prophecies. Only in hindsight can we interpret them. Jesus was born in Bethlehem, lived temporarily in Egypt, grew up in Nazareth, and lived and ministered in Capernaum, which was in the region of Naphtali and near the land of Zebulun.

Today, we have many prophetic voices that seem to contradict each other. And many in the body of Christ have become confused because they do not realize that prophecies can contradict each other and all come to pass.

That is why *prophecy* and not the *prophets* are to be judged by the body of Christ and other prophets. When all the parts come together, you have the complete revelation of the mystery.

> **Prophecies can contradict each other and all come to pass.**

Paul said, *"Love never ends. As for prophecies, they will pass away; as for tongues, they will cease; as for knowledge, it will pass away"* (1 Cor. 13:8 ESV).

When do prophecies pass away or become idle, as some Bibles translate that verse? When they are fulfilled. The prophecies about the coming Messiah were seeds sown by God's Word spoken by the power of the Holy Spirit through the mouths of His prophets. These seeds did not return void but accomplished exactly what God intended.

A seed is sown in the ground to produce a harvest, a fulfillment of a cycle. The proof of the seed is in your physical possession. By coming to fruition, the cycle is perfect, which is what Paul said. *"When the perfect comes, the partial will pass away"* (1 Cor. 13:10 ESV).

> **Prophecies are fulfilled whether or not you understand them.**

When we are fully mature and perfect, we won't need additional parts. We see a dim reflection now, only in parts. But when the body of Christ reaches the measure of the stature of the fullness of Christ and Jesus returns, we will see clearly and in high definition!

Sometimes You Can't Figure Out Prophecies

Prophecies are fulfilled whether or not you understand them. Just don't be left in the dust because a prophecy doesn't fit the framework of your mind.

You can easily see how the Jewish scribes, Pharisees, and others who were taught the Torah missed the Messiah's first coming. With seeming contradictions from the prophets, they adhered to the letter of the law and regulations and missed the Son of David, the Son of God, the Savior of the world. Prophecies are born of the Spirit, received by the spirit, and *understood spiritually.*

> **Prophecies are born of the Spirit, received by the spirit, and *understood spiritually.***

The Messiah was supposed to set up His kingdom and rule and reign forever. Instead, Jesus died on a cross, not having defeated Rome or the other enemies of God's chosen people, Israel. How could He be the Messiah?

Although the religious sector of Jesus' day was trained in the Torah, they looked for the Messiah in the way *they* thought He would come. The Messiah *did* come. But the part they missed is that He is coming twice.

In Jesus' first coming, He was born of a woman, preached righteousness, and healed people. His second coming will be with judgment at His appearing with *"countless thousands of his holy ones"* (Jude 1:14 NLT). *Then* He will set up His kingdom on the earth and rule forever.

The Messianic prophecies had more parts to them than the religious rulers had realized. And to be truthful, I don't think all the layers of the onion have been peeled back for our full view and understanding.

One thing is clear. Jesus is coming again! The prophecies go awry when prophets speak out of their minds, thoughts, and opinions rather than by the Spirit, or we try to interpret them by human reasoning.

Don't Miss the End-Time Move

We would be wise to heed this lesson lest we become trained in our minds about the way and manner in which God will manifest Himself to this generation. After all our churchgoing, praying, and reading the Bible, we must recognize the Holy Spirit's moving and manifestation and not miss the latter rain outpouring.

You ask, "How could we possibly miss it?"

In the 1970s, many denominations founded on the Word and the Spirit refused to recognize or participate in the Holy Spirit's outpouring on Catholics. Some said, "It couldn't possibly be of God because they are Catholic."

When my family grasped the principles of the Word of Faith, which changed our lives, the church my grandparents helped launch decades before asked us to leave. They excommunicated us because we followed the "dangerous" message of faith and healing.

> **He's not obligated to start a revival in a denomination or camp just because they were the first to get it the last time.**

God can move upon whomever He chooses. He's not obligated to start a revival in a denomination or camp just because they were the first to get it the last time. Expecting God to move in a similar way to the previous revival shows nothing but the limitations of our minds.

How will you recognize the outpouring of the Holy Spirit? Jesus' disciples followed Him because something in their hearts told them He was the Son of God. Their hearts leaped when He spoke, and their spirits were thrilled when He worked miracles.

The same will happen for you with the next move of God. Your heart will tell you, and your spirit will rejoice. You may see some things that aren't what you expected, but your spirit will bear witness that this is God moving.

CHAPTER 12

THE OLD AND THE NEW

It's time to expand our view of the prophetic. The concept of a prophet wearing animal skins, unshaven, unkempt, and prophesying with a loud voice, *Thus saith the Lord*, is dated, to say the least. It does seem, however, that some of these ideas are hard to get rid of.

I have noticed, to my dismay, that some groups of people ignore me unless I preface a prophetic word with *Thus saith the Lord* and raise my voice to a prophetic pitch.

I don't know how many times I had a true prophetic word that I shared in a church or in a private conversation that was met with a stare, or the person said, "Hmmm. Well, I gotta go now."

After being left standing there amazed a few times, I said, "Wow, God, that was a message for them, and they didn't even listen. That was *really* important stuff!"

> It's time to expand our view of the prophetic.

I was tempted to start using the "anointed" *Thus saith the Lord*, but the Spirit of God spoke to me and said, "They don't listen to Me either."

Three Prophetic Messages

A series of three prophetic messages came to me and were delivered over three years in specific succession. No one seemed to recognize the true meaning of these messages, including me. But I knew the prophetic anointing was preparing the body of Christ for something.

God's Third Choice

The first message, given to me in November of 2017, was called "God's Third Choice." When I was ministering, I knew this message was something more than a sermon and was somehow prophetic. I sensed it had broader applications than just ministering to the people in that service.

The message focused on the fact that King David was God's third choice for king. God had wanted to rule the children of Israel, but they said, "No. We want a man to be king and rule over us."

In other words, they wanted a human system of government instead of a spiritual system designed by their Creator. They rejected God and wanted a middleman. They were warned by the prophet Samuel that this would not work out well, but they had more faith in man's rule and government than in God.

Saul, in his arrogance, thought he could rule without God's direction and miserably failed.

I told the congregation that we don't always get our first choice, and neither does God. This may have shocked some of the listeners, but the evidence is clear.

God's first choice was to rule the Israelites Himself, and He was rejected outright. Saul was His second choice, and that didn't work out either. But God doesn't quit.

> They wanted a human system of government instead of a spiritual system designed by their Creator.

Even though God's plan doesn't turn out according to His perfect will chronologically, He keeps seeking those who will listen and obey Him. He found David, a man after His own heart. David loved God and eagerly sought His divine governance.

At first, David did not seem to be suitable material. Saul looked like a king—he was tall and had a presence about him. David was young, but God doesn't choose according to man's opinion. He looks at what is on the inside.

Israel rejected God, and Saul rejected God's guidance. But David sought God with his whole heart, and God finally found His man.

Things don't always work out the way we want or expect, but God still reigns in our hearts and in His kingdom. He will not quit until His final goal is reached. We can't allow ourselves to be discouraged when everything around us seems to be going the wrong way.

I have often thought of what the Holy Spirit said that night when the elections in the United States (2016 and 2020) did not turn out as many believers expected. What we were hearing from the Spirit of God that night was preparation for our preconceived ideas to be shaken. Our ideas may be shaken, but ultimately the plan of God will prevail.

> He will not quit until His final goal is reached.

David was the least likely of Jesse's sons to be chosen. It did not escape me that the mightiest move of God may well rest upon those the Church does not expect.

The Beginning of the Next Wave

In November 2018, as I prepared to minister at a Sunday morning church service in DeSoto, Kansas, I was moved into a prophetic anointing. I knew the anointing for that service would be different than the services I had previously ministered in.

Although I had flowed in the spirit of prophecy for quite some time in the 1980s, I gradually shifted into more of a teaching ministry with an occasional prophetic anointing. However, the Spirit came upon me that Sunday morning as I prayed in my hotel room before the service. In an instant, I knew the shift back to a prophetic anointing had come.

The message that morning was directed toward a Holy Spirit outpouring that was coming—a great move of the Holy Spirit that would surpass all previous revivals and awakenings.

The focus was shifting to Israel as the Gentile nations—specifically the United States—had held her cup full of the oil of the Spirit. The nations were waiting for the time to hand that precious gift back to God's chosen people in preparation for the return of the Messiah.

I shared with the congregation that morning the *old*. For the first time, I was led to share my testimony of being saved and how my sister and I were supernaturally baptized in the Holy Spirit. I was feeling the stirrings of the Spirit. The new move we had prayed for was in the beginning stage.

Escaping Gravity

The third message was in November 2019. "Escaping Gravity" came to me in a visual way. I saw in my spirit a representation of the earth and its orbit around the sun.

The earth is caught in the sun's gravitational field and will continue in its orbit unless an outside force knocks it out of orbit. I could literally see in the spirit something like a large asteroid hurtling from the darkness of the galaxy, hitting the earth, and changing its orbit. I did not interpret this as literal but symbolic.

All of us have something in our lives that we rotate around. It could be family, work, church, or a hobby. Something exerts a gravitational pull on us and keeps us orbiting around it. It's only when something unexpectedly hits us and knocks us out of orbit that we reexamine the reality of our lives and where we are going from there.

It could be a toxic relationship for some people, and no matter how hard they try, they can't seem to break free. Others are dedicated to their jobs, and their entire life is focused on work. Some parents orbit around their children, and it is a difficult change when the child leaves home and their center of orbit is no longer there.

In 2007 and again in 2021, the people of New Orleans and Louisiana's coastal areas were uprooted when a hurricane destroyed the structure of their lives. They were forced to move, find new housing and new jobs. They were knocked out of the structured orbit of their lives.

> **It's only when something unexpectedly hits us and knocks us out of orbit that we reexamine the reality of our lives.**

In our nation, our culture is built upon the concept of freedom that produces a tremendous supply of prosperity—meaning an abundant supply of food and products is available upon demand.

I could see something was coming that would metaphorically knock the earth out of its everyday orbit.

Little did I know that a virus would disrupt every society and nation on the earth, and the concept of freedom we have revolved around would be called into question. The supply of food and products we have come to depend on disappeared, and grocery store shelves were almost empty.

That prophetic message was meant to prepare us for the changes that were coming. It was meant to remind us that the only thing we should be orbiting around is God's Word and His Kingdom, not man. Our dependence should only be on the Holy Spirit to guide us. The Word of God is our foundation and the only thing that cannot be shaken!

What of the Future?

Will the future be full of darkness or full of light? Both.

The prophets of old—dressed in strange clothing—have prophesied that the forces of darkness would be unleashed upon the earth in the time of the end. It has also been prophesied that *"the people who know their God shall be strong, and carry out great exploits"* (Dan. 11:32 NKJV).

The body of Christ has yet to reach its full potential and stand empowered by the Spirit, demonstrating signs and wonders to the world, but we will.

We must first learn from the past and those who have kept alive the words of Jesus to heal the sick, cast out devils, and raise the dead. Every generation has had a breaking through of the Spirit and some manifestation of the gifts of the Holy Spirit.

> **Each revival and outpouring has built upon the others.**

Each revival and outpouring has built upon the others. The Azusa Street Revival and the Pentecostal outpouring at the turn of the 20th century, the healing revivals of the 1950s, the Jesus Movement of the 1960s, the Charismatic Renewal and Word of Faith Movement of the 1970s and 1980s were divine visitations.

Old and New Wineskins

As with each movement before, new wineskins to hold the new wine are needed. We are called to follow the cloud of the Spirit. When the Spirit moves, it's necessary to go where He goes. That means being called out. Called out of your current orbit, which may be your denomination, church, religious dogma, or whatever "movement" you belong to.

Animal skin clothing and eating locusts don't work for today's society. But much more than clothing has changed. We are on a collision course of the old and new.

What happened in the past is to be built upon, not worshiped. We really have no concept of how God will intervene in this generation. To be sure, they will reject the structure and concepts of their parents' generation and forge a new way.

If we allow them to experience the Spirit and knowledge of the Word that came through the prophets of old, they will lead their generation to the final destination.

Jesus being baptized by John the Baptist in the Jordan River was a great contrast between the old and new. Both individuals were divinely born, announced by angels, and fulfilled the will of the Father.

As John baptized people in the wilderness, he looked every bit like the wild prophets of old when he shouted, *"Repent!"*

Jesus, on the other hand, may have come to the Jordan River wearing the fine garment the soldiers cast lots for when He was later crucified. The Son of Man came up out of the water with the Spirit descending on Him. Jesus, the prophet, healed the sick and held little children in the love of God.

Such a contrast. Both were anointed and called. One from the old way of traditions and the other from a new and living way.

During the last days, some prophets will speak and behave like Elijah did—prophesying against the darkness. And we will also have the gentle healing touch of Jesus through the gifts of the healings. It has been foretold that the spirit of prophecy will come upon children and men and women.

So where are we going? I have shared the old from my experiences with the Spirit

> We are on a collision course of the old and new.

> **The prophecy is still waiting for those who will receive it.**

of God. I want to now share prophetic utterances that came through my father, Charles Capps. Some of the prophetic words are being fulfilled now. Some have come to pass in a small way, but the prophecy is still waiting for those who will receive it.

Listen closely. Pay attention and don't be like the folks who said, "Hmmm," and walked off. It's up to you to listen and heed the call.

CHAPTER 13

PROPHETIC WORDS
GIVEN THROUGH CHARLES CAPPS

THE TRIANGLE OF THE END

July 1987

"There shall be great manifestations of My Spirit."

Those who prophesy doom have seen some things, but they haven't seen it all. They say that darkness is coming, and darkness is overshadowing. Yet, in the same time frame, there will be a great light and great manifestations of My power.

For as you approach the triangle of the end, time shall grow closer. Time shall grow closer and faster because it is coming to a point. And it must be line upon line, precept upon precept down the middle of this triangle. Time shall go faster and closer, faster and closer, faster and closer.

There was a day when at the top of the triangle, you could be way to one side, following afar off and still be in the light that is inside the triangle.

Outside this triangle is darkness—gross darkness—and it shall cover the earth. The world shall walk in that darkness. But my people are inside the triangle, and the light is growing lighter.

The light is coming to a point until it becomes a laser. At that point, the light shall be bright. The light shall manifest more. Illumination shall bring more understanding.

So the line that comes down the center of the triangle is My Word—precept upon precept, line upon line. The one who followed afar off several years ago was still in the light. But as you get to the little end of the triangle, that person will be in darkness, gross darkness.

Gird up your loins with the truth. Draw close to My Word. Polarize yourself with the Word of God. Let the entrance of the Word illuminate you. Come as close to that Word and that perfection as you can. For I have said in My Word, *"Be ye perfect, even as I am perfect."*

Strive to come in line with the Word that you may grow up into all things in Christ. For the darkness and the wicked spirits have sped up their activities—faster, faster, faster, and closer. And so have I sped up My activities in the triangle of light for more illumination, more illumination.

For you have seen the illumination that is coming, but you have not seen the manifestation of My power that shall be at the end of the triangle. For it will be light, then lighter, and brighter. Then it becomes a laser, and there shall be a great manifestation of my power.

Commentary

As the apostle Paul instructed the church at Corinth, the gift of prophecy edifies, exhorts, and comforts. "The Triangle of the End" was given in 1987 and explicitly reveals that both great light and great darkness will exist in the same time frame. It exhorts us to stay close to God and His Word.

Included in the prophecy is a line that states, "Time shall grow closer and faster." Does anyone living in this era of technology not have the sensation that this is true? Since prophecies are often layered, there may be other pieces to this prophecy that will be revealed.

At the time it was given, I could see glimpses of this concept. But never in my imagination would I have considered the great darkness that would come upon the nation and world by the year 2020. And yet, revival has begun, with greater light and illumination of the Word than I ever thought possible.

How would you describe your relationship with God? Are you following afar off? Or is your heart and mind tuned in daily to hear the Word of the Lord to you?

Draw near to God and He will draw near to you.
James 4:8 NKJV

But as for me, it is good to draw near to God. I have made the Lord God my refuge, that I may proclaim all Your works.
Psalm 73:28

WALK IN THE ANOINTING

July 1987

"You will walk in the wisdom of God when others are stumbling and falling to the wayside."

Have I not said that if you will hearken diligently unto the voice of the Lord your God and observe to do all that is written therein, then all of these blessings shall come upon you? And they shall overtake you.

They shall come from behind and move faster than you are. In any way you are going, they will run you down. And the anointing of God shall cause the manifestation of the power of God.

As I said to the children of Israel, how much more is it now in this day under the New Covenant that you will be blessed coming in and going out, in the basket and in the store?

And as I said to Joshua of old, "Let not this Word depart from your mouth, but meditate therein day and night."

Mutter the Word to yourself. Say it to yourself. Speak it to yourself. And as David said, "I spoke to my heart upon my bed." Meditate. And as David said, "Write these things by the pen of my lips upon my heart."

Oh, in this day, if men will use and walk in the anointing of God and see the invisible things that are clearly revealed.

There will be turmoil. There will be strife. There will be darkness on every side. But you will walk in the light of life. And you will walk in the wisdom of God when others are stumbling and falling to the wayside, saying, "How are they doing it?"

You will walk in divine provision. For My Word has set it forth in the midst of you. Now bring it into your heart, plant it in the soil, and walk with Me. And we together shall win.

Commentary

Again, we are warned that there will be turmoil, strife, and darkness. However, those who walk with God and heed His voice will receive His wisdom and divine provision during these times.

It is important for us to realize that to be "overtaken" by the blessings of God, we must *choose* to walk with Him, speak and meditate on His Word, and be a *doer* of Jesus' sayings. How can we be a "doer of the Word"? We start by declaring God's Word aloud and saying what *He says* about us.

> *Be doers of the word, and not hearers only. Otherwise, you are deceiving yourselves.*
>
> James 1:22

IF YOU WILL ALLOW ME, I WILL PULL DOWN STRONGHOLDS THROUGH YOUR VOICE

October 1980

"I will intercede through your voice, and I will pull down the strongholds of the enemy, and My church shall rise and walk in victory."

My people have staggered, stumbled, and walked in little light in days past. For you see, the light had not come to its fullness. They walked in what light had been revealed.

But the day is at hand when the light shall come in a brightness that no man has ever seen or understood. It is time now, and My people shall rise to their feet clothed with the righteousness of God.

My anointing shall flow in them and bring forth the manifestation of My power. For it shall be by this means that the intercessor shall pull down strongholds and break the powers of darkness.

Whole cities and nations shall be brought into the Kingdom because of intercession that shall come out of the spirits of men by the Holy Spirit. For I will intercede for the nations of the world.

If My people would but allow Me, I shall pull down strongholds, for I shall cut down imaginations and every high thing. For My words are powerful words, and I shall speak as the Most High, and it shall come through your voice.

No man, no nation, and no enemy shall be able to stand against it. You have already seen it come to pass in this nation. You saw it in the election in November 1980, for My people have cried out to Me and allowed Me to intercede for this nation.

As ye continue to yield yourself and as more light comes, the nations of the world shall stand in awe at what I will do. For I will intercede through your voice. And I shall pull down the strongholds of the enemy, and My Church shall rise and walk in victory.

I shall come for a glorious Church. So learn to walk in the light of what has been revealed, and I will reveal more light. And you shall be a blessed generation that shall see these things come to pass.

For the intercession that comes from within flows from the wisdom of God and from the hearts of men. You shall intercede and pray for things that men do not know are even in the making. But you shall call them into being and shall pull down things that have been planned for years to destroy God's people.

Even though you do not know they are there, if you allow Me, I will make them to become nothing through your spirit, through your words.

For My spirit is upon you and in you and flowing through you, and the rivers of water that come are waters of life.

Not only will they pull down the strongholds of the enemy, but they shall bring into the Kingdom new light and new life.

And My people shall have a harvest in the days of the end like no people on the earth have ever seen.

For the days are at hand that I shall move mightily on the earth, but it will be by the Spirit. It will be by the anointing. It will not be by natural means, by natural learning, by natural understanding.

For the wisdom that will flow through the spirits of men will be so far beyond the carnal mind that no man can comprehend or understand.

But the Spirit of the Lord shall move mightily through My people, and so shall My words. The words shall come forth. The word shall be the Word of the Lord. The word shall be the Words of God. And the Word shall bring down strongholds.

My Word will bring in those who are out in the darkness, and light shall come in the midst of darkness.

Some of you have allowed the enemy to steal your loved ones and steal from you. If you would have allowed Me, I would have interceded on your behalf, and My words shall not return unto Me void. They will accomplish that whereunto I send them.

But because of a lack of understanding, some of you have become weary of speaking a language you did not understand. Not knowing and understanding that you were releasing spiritual forces and power beyond what any enemy could understand.

For it is out of your belly that flow rivers of living waters that shall come like a flood tide and shall sweep away the adversary and bring to pass the prophecies of My Word.

Gird up your loins with the knowledge of the truth that has been revealed and walk with Me, and I will walk with you. And I will speak through you and intercede through you. Allow Me, and we together shall win.

Commentary

God desires to pull down the strongholds of wickedness. And He does so through men and women who intercede by the anointing of the Holy Spirit. He uses their voices as they allow. Will you yield yourself to the Spirit to "call things that be not" and "break down the strongholds" of the enemy?

> *He saw that there was no man; He was amazed that there was no one to intercede. So His own arm brought salvation, and His own righteousness sustained Him.*
>
> Isaiah 59:16

> *The weapons of our warfare are not the weapons of the world. Instead, they have divine power to demolish strongholds.*
>
> 2 Corinthians 10:4

Likewise the Spirit helps us in our weakness. For we do not know what to pray for as we ought, but the Spirit himself intercedes for us with groanings too deep for words.

Romans 8:26 ESV

FINANCIAL INVERSION

February 1, 1978

Honolulu, Hawaii

"The reservoirs of the wicked shall be tapped and shall be drained into the gospel of Jesus Christ."

Financial inversions shall come forth from this that has been wrought tonight. So shall it be that even the smallest that has been set forth in motion here shall not be forgotten. It shall be multiplied.

Financial inversion shall increase in these days. For you see, it is My desire to move in the realm of your financial prosperity. But release Me, saith the Lord. Release Me that I may come in on your behalf and move on your behalf.

For yes, there shall be in this hour financial distress here and there. The economy shall go up, and it will go down. But those who learn to walk in the Word shall see the prosperity of the Word come forth in this hour in a way that has not been seen by men in days past.

Yes, there is coming a financial inversion in the world's system. It's been held in the reservoirs of wicked men for days on end. But the end is nigh.

Those reservoirs shall be tapped and shall be drained into the Gospel of Jesus Christ. It shall be done in the time allotted. And so shall it be that the word of the Lord shall come to pass that the wealth of the sinner is laid up for the just.

Predominantly, in two ways shall it be done in this hour. Those who have hoarded up and stored because of the inspiration of the evil one and held the money from the Gospel shall be converted and drawn into the Kingdom. And then shall it release that reservoir into the Kingdom.

But many, many will not. They will not heed the voice of the Word of God. They will turn aside to this, and they will turn to that, and they will walk in their own ways. But their ways will not work in this hour.

It will dwindle, and it will slip away as though it were in bags with holes in them. It will go here, and it will go there. And they will wonder why it's not working now. "It worked in days past," they will say.

But it shall be, saith the Lord, that the word of the Lord shall rise within men—men of God of low esteem in the financial world—who shall claim the Word of God to be their very own and walk in the light of it as it has been set forth in the Word and give.

They will begin to give small at first because that's all they have. But then it will increase.

And through the hundredfold return, so shall it be that the reservoirs that have held the riches in days past shall return it to the hands of the giver. Because of the hundredfold return shall the reservoirs be lost from the wicked and turned to the Gospel.

For it shall be in this hour that you will see things you have never dreamed come to pass. Oh, it will be strong at first in ways. Then it will grow greater and greater until men will be astounded. The world will stand in awe because the ways of men have failed, and the ways of God shall come forth.

As men walk in My Word, so shall they walk in the ways of the Lord. Oh yes, there will be some who say, "Yes, but God's ways are higher, surely higher than our ways, and we can't walk in those."

It's true that the ways of God are higher. They are higher than your ways as the heavens are above the earth, but I will teach you to walk in My ways. I never did say you could not walk in My ways.

Now learn to walk in it. Learn to give. So shall the inversion of the financial system revert, and so shall it be that the Gospel of the kingdom shall be preached to all the world, and there shall be no lack in the kingdom.

Those who give shall walk in the ways of the supernatural, and they shall be known abroad. My Word shall spread, and the knowledge of the Lord shall fill all the earth in the day and the hour in which ye stand. Ye shall see it and know it, for it is of Me, and it shall come to pass, saith the Lord.

Commentary

This prophecy, which was given in 1978, has been widely circulated. As I was reading it again, I became convinced that many people (including myself) have shouted and praised God over this excitedly, thinking it would just fall on us as believers without any action on our part. I have heard the following scripture quoted many times:

> *A good man leaveth an inheritance to his children's children: and the wealth of the sinner is laid up for the just.*
>
> **Proverbs 13:22 KJV**

People of faith often comment to me, "Isn't it great? All that wealth will come to us who are believers!" Yes, it's great, but there is something *we* must do!

The Spirit of God is telling us in this prophetic word that this wealth will come primarily in (but not limited to) two ways:

1. The conversion of the wealthy wicked who will begin to give according to kingdom principles.

2. The wealthy wicked will begin to lose their hold on the money they have hoarded.

What action is required of us? Pray for laborers to be sent (and be willing to do so ourselves) to take the light of Jesus Christ to all people, including the wealthy.

Are you praying for the salvation of all men as Paul instructed? The Bible way to our own prosperity is giving and giving with faith attached to the promise of God.

Are you doing your part by giving, even if you start small? Are you believing for a hundredfold return so you can give even more to the kingdom of God and the needy?

And God is able to make all grace abound to you, so that in all things, at all times, having all that you need, you will abound in every good work.

2 Corinthians 9:8

DRAINING THE FINANCIAL RESERVOIRS OF THE WICKED

1981

*"My people shall walk in love, in power,
and in prosperity in the latter end."*

I desire to reveal to My people the secrets of wisdom and authority of My Word. As they walk in the light of what they have and begin to operate in the principles of My Word, life shall come forth that shall be beyond what men have seen in days past.

An understanding of wisdom in the area of finances will come until men shall walk in an avenue of understanding, and the world shall be astounded. They shall say, "How are they doing it? How do they manage to come up with this?"

It will be so that as these walk in the hundredfold return principle, it shall drain the reservoirs of wicked men. For the Word of the Lord will come alive on the earth.

The Word shall come in the midst of this nation, and you will see it rise to its feet. My people shall walk in love, in power, and in prosperity in the latter end because they have learned My Word and walk in My ways.

Oh, there will be some that will try to walk in it and gain great riches for their own purpose. But they will fail; they will fail. And it will not work for them at all.

But they that will walk in the precepts of My Word, be diligent and be obedient to it—it shall be that they shall prosper and shall finance this Gospel around the world.

Further and further shall it be from what men have done in days past. They shall say that it has never been and never shall be. *But it will be!* In this generation, and My people shall do it, for I am revealing the secrets of My Word.

Be not afraid of sudden fear, neither of the desolation of the wicked when it cometh. For the Lord shall be thy confidence and shall keep thy foot from being taken.

These things that are coming on the earth today are not designed to do My people in, but to cause them to walk in the life that I reveal in My Word.

The desolation of the wicked is at hand, for the wicked shall be cut off on the earth. But the knowledge of the Lord shall spread throughout the earth through My Word, and men shall walk in the wisdom of God.

And the knowledge of God shall cause My people to triumph in the desolation of the wicked. So shall they stand in the midst and shall come as shining lights in the midst of a dark generation.

My light shall grow brighter. Their darkness shall grow darker, and My truth shall be revealed in all the earth!

Commentary

Similar to the "Financial Inversion" prophecy, notice that an understanding of God's wisdom in the area of finances is required. God's wisdom and man's wisdom are often far apart.

To man's wisdom, giving $100 makes him $100 poorer. Conversely, Jesus said, *"Give, and it shall be given unto you"* (Luke 6:38 KJV).

When operating in the principles of the Kingdom of God, you give and are many times richer than before you gave. This is the principle of the seed. A seed does not produce one more seed; it produces many seeds.

God's laws of giving and receiving are self-enforcing and based on His ways, which are pure. Look at the line, "There will be some who will try to walk in it and gain great riches for their own purpose. But they will fail, and it will not work for them at all."

Greed and covetousness produce after their kind, and the results are *not* the blessing of God. Riches gained that way will slip away.

Are you seeking the wisdom of God for your personal finances?

Is your heart in your giving, and are you prepared to receive financial blessings in return?

> *Now He who supplies seed to the sower and bread for food will supply and multiply your store of seed and will increase the harvest of your righteousness. You will be enriched in every way to be generous on every occasion, so that through us your giving will produce thanksgiving to God.*
>
> 2 Corinthians 9:10-11

THIS NATION WILL BE REVIVED

November 29, 1980

"I have heard the cry of My people,
and I will answer."

This nation is not going down the drain. This nation will rise to its feet and will prevail in the day when all the world will say, "How can it survive?"

It will. It will, for I will move mightily in this nation. For My people have sought Me. My people have come to Me, and I have heard their voice—the cry of My people—and I will answer. I have already answered, and I will continue to answer.

For My people shall gird up their loins, and they will preach My Word. They will speak My Word, and they will pull down spiritual wickedness in high places.

I have an army, and they are coming forth in this hour. They are coming forth with wisdom and power. They are coming in waves of hundreds and thousands and even millions. They will prevail on the earth.

This nation will rise to its feet. This nation will come alive. This nation will revive. So intercede and speak, and I will move mightily. And you will see it in your day.

Commentary

Much discussion and prophesying have been done in the past few years concerning the condition of our nation. Because of the turmoil and chaos that seems to have overtaken our land and our society, many have become disheartened and depressed concerning the future of the United States.

Although this prophecy was given in 1980, prophecy has no expiration date, and I urge you to allow this word to give you hope.

Again, believers have a part to play in this scenario: *"My people have sought Me, and I have heard the cry of My people."*

Even as far back as 1980, people were troubled and discouraged at the direction of the nation. But God never fails to hear the voice of His people when they intercede and seek Him.

> *If my people, which are called by my name, shall humble themselves, and pray, and seek my face, and turn from their wicked ways; then will I hear from heaven, and will forgive their sin, and will heal their land.*
> 2 Chronicles 7:14 KJV

The things that take place in this nation are influenced by prayer or lack thereof. Because change comes slowly most of the time, we haven't made the connection that the nation is suffering from our lack of sincere prayer and intercession.

When things are going well, we think we have prayed enough. When the nation is in crisis, we wonder why God is not answering our prayers immediately. In reality, the prosperity of the nation may be the result of much prayer 10 years before.

Are you diligent to pray and intercede for our nation even when there is peace and prosperity?

Do you seek God and show up to vote?

We must be vigilant and guard God's plan for this nation that she completely fulfills her calling by using every right and privilege God has given us.

MY ARMY WILL BE INVOLVED IN THE GOVERNMENTS

July 11, 1980

Minneapolis, Minnesota

*"I am marshaling My forces, and the politicians
are seeing the handwriting on the wall."*

In days past, it has been very unpopular in government circles to mention religious or born-again experiences. But in the day in which you live, it will be more popular to say, "I am born again," than to speak against the God of all creation.

For you see, I am raising up an army, and they are beginning to stand up now. They have sat on the sidelines in days past, but I am marshaling My forces.

And the politicians are seeing the handwriting on the wall. The government and things of the world shall be changed because the men who come into leadership shall be ordained of God, for My people are coming together.

Some would say, "Oh, how will it ever be so? We are so outnumbered."

No, you're not! In the days to come as the world walks on in darkness, their darkness shall grow darker, and their understanding shall be dimmed.

Because they are approaching the kingdom of darkness, their darkness shall become gross darkness. They will not know where to turn. They will stumble and fall, and they will not know at what they stumble.

But My people who are called by My Name who walk in the light of My Word, as they approach the end of time, they are coming closer to the kingdom of light.

Their light shall grow lighter. Their wisdom shall grow more profound. They will be able to look and see all around. They will see every obstacle. They will step to this side and to that side.

They will be able to solve problems that no others have been able to solve. And the world will say, "Who are these who seem to know how to perform such miracles as we have heard about in days past?"

They are Mine! My army that I am raising up will be involved in governments. They will change multitudes. For when the kings served other gods, so did all Israel go astray.

So lift up your heads and rejoice! For that which is before you is your choice! And I will move mightily to see that the choice is right. Lift up your heads and rejoice, for I am doing a new thing on the earth.

Commentary

God has put out a call to His people to *get involved!* No more standing around. No more hiding in fear. It is time to step into the light with the wisdom God has given you and find *divine solutions.*

Many have wanted to stay out of the local, state, and federal governments because they didn't want to get their hands dirty with politics. Yes, it is a filthy place because of what we have allowed in.

Where are our Holy Spirit anointed men and women on the school boards? In the city and county government offices of authority?

Are you willing to say, *"Here am I, Lord, send me"*?

You may not go to the U.S. Senate (or maybe so), but you are surrounded with numerous local government structures that need your light shining in the darkness.

Will you *go* where He sends you?

> Then I heard the voice of the Lord saying: *"Whom shall I send? Who will go for Us?"* And I said: *"Here am I. Send me!"*
>
> Isaiah 6:8

SUPERNATURAL MANIFESTATIONS OF MINISTERING SPIRITS

November 27, 1980

*"Mighty battles shall be won because of the
supernatural element in the days to come."*
*"My last move throughout the earth will
marshal all of the forces of the universe."*

In the days to come, you are going to see supernatural manifestations of the ministering spirits of God throughout the nations of this world.

You have already seen it in this nation. You have seen it in the [1980] election. You have seen it in the things that have turned about in the last few months in this nation.

It has not come by chance. It has not come by some man. It has come supernaturally because My people have interceded. My people have spoken. My people have set things in motion by words and agreed with Me. They cooperated with the Spirit of God.

I have moved mightily on the earth, and so shall I continue to move in this nation—not only this nation but in the nations of the world. There will come great and supernatural manifestations of the power through ministering spirits on the earth in the latter days.

So begin now to look into the things I have shared in My Word, for they will come to the forefront in these days. They will come gradually—a little at a time, a little at a time here, and a little there. They will happen in this nation and that nation.

There will come a great explosion of supernatural manifestations, and the ministering spirits shall minister supernaturally. Mighty battles shall be won because of the supernatural element.

In the days to come, you will see it and know that it was of My Spirit and My Power. For I shall move mightily on the earth, and the nations of the world will stand in awe.

For I am not through on this earth. I will bring forth the manifestation of My wisdom and My knowledge throughout this earth. And oh yes, there is going to be supernatural deliverance for people in the nations of the world, and you will see it.

There will be some, it will look like there is no way out—that they will be totally destroyed, annihilated. But because of the supernatural intervention of the ministering spirits and supernatural deliverance, those governments will be changed. Nations will be changed.

Governments will be moved upon throughout the nations of the world, and they will call for a prophet. "Send us someone who will teach us about these things we have seen. We don't understand them, but we would desire to know more about them."

And the prophets will go, and they will prevail. And nations of the world will be changed. And places that looked like they would never come under the Gospel will be those that will promote the Gospel throughout the nations of the world. You will see it and know it, for I will perform it, saith the Lord.

Don't think it strange that these things have been reserved for the latter end. For you see, they came in days of old, and they came forth in many of the prophets of God.

But you will see them in the days to come on a greater and a higher plain. For you see, I have saved the best for last. And My last move throughout the earth will marshal all the forces of the universe of the Spirit of God to work these things out. They will come forth.

They will be busily about in this nation bringing forth the things that My people are interceding for. For your intercession has not gone unnoticed, saith the Lord. For you have already seen some of it come to pass. But you have only seen the tip of the iceberg that is about to rise and float to the surface and move throughout this nation and spread to other nations of the world.

The mighty move of My Spirit shall bring the world to their knees, and they shall confess Jesus as Lord, for I shall move mightily, and nations of the world shall be changed. Revival shall sweep totally throughout the land because of things that will come to pass in these days, saith the Lord.

Commentary

Where do I begin to comment on this profound word from the Lord? That the angels will play a tremendous part in the last days is without question once you have read the book of Revelation.

The angels bring supernatural deliverance for the literal descendants of Abraham and those of us Gentiles who have been grafted in. Angels are called ministering spirits:

> *Are they not all ministering spirits, sent forth to minister for them who shall be heirs of salvation?*
>
> **Hebrews 1:14 KJV**

That they have been involved in the supernatural deliverance of Daniel from the lions' den and Peter from prison shows us their involvement in the affairs of mankind.

> *For he shall give his angels charge over thee, to keep thee in all thy ways.*
>
> **Psalm 91:11 KJV**

Angels are also loosed to bring judgment and destruction upon the wicked. Balaam was met by an angel with a sword who was sent to kill him.

Angels play a part in putting people in positions of government and removing them at God's direction.

From this prophecy, it appears that there will be some outstanding supernatural occurrences from the ministry of angels in the end times. So what can we do to participate?

Angels respond to words, so be sure that the words of your mouth are in agreement with God's Word. Don't start poor-mouthing and crying when you see outstanding acts take place. God is cleaning up the mess!

Will you use your words and your prayers on behalf of those blinded by satan by using your authority to break the power of darkness over their lives?

(For more information on angels, visit our website or any bookstore for *Angels: Knowing Their Purpose, Releasing Their Power*.)

THE AVENUES OF THE SPIRIT

July 1978

"So shall the anointing of God team up with you,
and so shall we work together to prevail."
"Evil will be cast forth and the Word of the
Lord will have dominion on the earth."

The avenues of My Spirit are limitless. So are the avenues of man's spirit. They are limitless.

The horizons that are before you are horizons of new frontiers that men who will walk in the Word will enter. The world has looked and said, "There are none. The frontiers are all gone."

They are not all gone. The frontiers of the Spirit are coming into their own in this hour. Learn to walk in the ways of the Word. Learn to speak the things you have heard from the Word. Learn to be obedient to My laws, and My Spirit will move inside your spirit.

We together will overcome, and we will walk in the power of the Spirit. We will walk in My wisdom. We will walk together, and we will be as one.

Those that say darkness is coming and doom shall prevail have only to read My Word and find that satan shall not prevail. Darkness has never prevailed over light. Neither shall it be that darkness shall ever prevail in the presence of light.

For the entrance of the Word bringeth light, and the light shall drive out the darkness. Darkness shall flee. Darkness shall not penetrate any light, but the light shall penetrate all darkness.

So allow My Spirit to move within you. Allow your spirit freedom to release yourself in My Word. Release your spirit. Release yourself. Allow Me to move on your behalf, for I desire to move for My People.

I desire to create better things for My people. And the Word of the Lord shall prevail. The Word of the Lord will not fail. The Word of the Lord shall be the only thing that will stand.

The earth shall shake. The earth shall tremble. Everything that can be shaken will be shaken in the end.

Stand upon My Word, for My Word shall never fall. It will never fail. When all else fails, My Word shall stand.

So don't turn and look to the wisdom or authority of man, but look to My Word. Understand My Word. Seek the Kingdom. Seek the knowledge of My Word. Apply it in the midst of your spirit.

So shall the anointing of God team up with you, and so shall we work together to prevail. So shall the evil be cast forth. So shall the Word of the Lord have dominion on the earth.

When the Lord comes, will He find that kind of faith upon the earth? It shall be so. It shall be that this faith shall prevail.

The enemy shall fail, but the one who walks in faith shall prevail.

Commentary

What's out there in the realm of the Spirit that we haven't tapped? What realms of heaven's resources have we not entered into because of complacency? Have we reached the end of the frontier of exploration of the things of God? I think not.

Our bodies and minds may be limited, but our spirits are not! They are eternal and made in the image and likeness of God. When we turn to human reasoning, we enter a very limited resource, and we can see the results of that action in the world today.

By searching the things of the Spirit, and the revelation of the Word, we change *ourselves* first. Darkness and confusion will not prevail over those who pursue the avenues of the Spirit in the Kingdom of God.

The way to triumph over darkness is to introduce light. Fighting against darkness will get you nowhere, but by simply introducing light, darkness is driven back. The apostle Paul also instructed us to overcome the darkness of evil with good.

> *Do not be overcome and conquered by evil, but overcome evil with good.*
>
> Romans 12:21 AMP

The solutions to the world's problems today and the challenges in your life lie within the light of God's Word and the illumination of the Spirit. Divine solutions lie within the avenues of the Spirit—our spirit divinely connected to the Holy Spirit. By praying in the Spirit, we can enter the riches of God's resources and find wisdom to meet every situation.

God's Word is not religious dogma that ensnares us into repetitive practices that mean nothing. God's Word is *alive* and *living*. This living force enters our minds and hearts, allowing us to enter the limitless avenues of the Spirit.

Are you hungry for God in your heart to discover new avenues and frontiers of the Spirit? Are you ready to move forward and introduce light into the darkness and prevail?

SEQUENCE, TIMING, AND FULFILLMENT

June 26, 1989

England, Arkansas

"There is a sequence of events that must gravitate naturally in the timing of God for fulfillment."

In the world, there is a sequence of events that gravitate toward the timing of Almighty God to bring forth the fulfillment and manifestation of the events prophesied in the days before.

So is it, even in this nation, that a sequence of events have already started and are gravitating toward the timing of the end. You see it on the horizon; you see it in the newspapers daily.

There must be a gravitation toward that timing. For the sequence of these events must correlate to God's timing to bring forth the fulfillment and manifestation of end-time events prophesied by the prophets of old.

In your individual life also, there is a sequence of events that must gravitate naturally to the timing of God for fulfillment. Some of the things you have seen are for the days to come. Every individual has a sequence of events that must transpire in the natural order of gravitation toward the timing of God.

If you force that and get out of the sequence of events by pressing into the spirit realm to force a manifestation, then you break out of God's timing and reach into the world of the spirit with which you are not familiar. And some of these spirits will deceive you and lead you astray into a realm that is not for the order of the day.

But if you allow the natural gravitation of these events—which will come by the anointing of God within you to lead you in these things—then it will be in perfect timing. Even as an automobile has a timing chain that will keep the sequence of that engine in perfect timing to power it forward, so it is in the life of every individual.

Be careful that you don't press the order of events that have been revealed to you either by revelation, by knowledge, or by your spirit. But allow—through prayer in the Spirit and with the understanding also—the gravitation unto the sequence of those events, and it will come in perfect timing. In the days to come, you will live out the reality of that thing in a natural flow of the Spirit of God.

But be careful that you don't press into that realm of the spirit trying to operate on someone else's anointing, lest you encounter a realm of the spirit that you are not able to deal with because of timing. Some ministries have pushed into this realm through natural means, rather than in the Spirit.

They caught a glimpse, a revelation of My plan, will, and purpose, but they shifted over into the natural. They tried to force this by their natural initiative.

By their own initiative, they are forcing into the realm of the Spirit. By doing so, they open themselves to other spirits. That is why some ministries have fallen and others will fail.

Many are led astray, and they lead many astray. There is a sequence, a timing, and a fulfillment. And if you will allow it in your life, you won't have to struggle. You won't have to worry. You won't have to fret. You won't have to wring your hands in despair. But you will lift up your voice and rejoice because you will know the fulfillment is near.

But let it come by the Spirit of God, by the anointing of God, and by the flow of God. And then you will look back in the days to come and say, "I'm so glad that I was led by the Spirit and didn't get over into the natural." You will see these things in manifestation in the days to come in My timing and in the manifestation of My power in your individual lives.

Commentary

This prophecy is both a warning and an encouragement. How many of us get tired of waiting and push forward, only to find out that we missed it! We may have the vision, the determination, and the drive to get it done, but God's timing is ultimately important.

Moses wanted to deliver his people from oppression. He was called by God to lead the nation of Israel out of Egypt. But rather than letting things move on naturally until the timing was right, he stepped in and slew an Egyptian and became a fugitive in the desert for a long time!

In reading the wisdom of this prophecy, it seems to apply to my life every day. When we want something, we want it *now*. It pays to get into the Word and wait on God until He gives you the signal to take action.

What we are seeing in the world today is exactly what the prophets saw thousands of years ago, whether or not they understood it. We may not fully understand the progression and nuances of the end of the age, but there is a timing to it.

The glorious Church may enter into realms of glory that we haven't imagined, and there is a timing to that also. We cannot force it. The cloud of God's glory goes before us, and we are to follow.

Are you tuned into the voice of the Holy Spirit and only going where He leads?

> *To everything there is a season, and a time for every purpose under heaven.*
>
> **Ecclesiastes 3:1**

I AM RAISING UP SPECIALISTS IN AREAS OF MINISTRY

May 1980

*"A glorious Church that shall rise
in the midst of chaos."*

Truths of wisdom shall be opened in the latter days as though it were a fountain from above, a knowledge and understanding beyond the capacity of any human to perceive or comprehend.

For the fountain of knowledge and wisdom of God shall flow on the earth. It shall cover the earth as the sea doth cover the ocean floor. So shall the knowledge of My Word flow on the earth in a divine flow.

The anointing shall rest in one area, and the anointing shall flow to another area. Enlightenment shall come in that one area until it shall be magnified.

Then it shall explode as it were in the midst of the earth and shall be sent throughout the earth to proclaim and bring forth the manifestation of My power.

Then My Spirit shall move to another area. And then shall enlightenment come to that area, even as a soft glow at first. Understanding shall increase *and increase **and increase*** until it shall become as a brilliant light that shines from the throne of God to the hearts of men and illuminate the spirits of men. It shall bypass intellectual learning and go in depth to the spirits of men, causing them to walk in avenues of My wisdom.

Oh yes, My ways are higher than your ways. But I will teach you My ways if you will walk in My precepts. I will guide you into divine truths.

For these are the days of mighty manifestations of My power. These are the days of the manifestation of God on the earth as men have not known before.

For I shall minister on the earth through My creation, through My wisdom, a divine flow into the hearts of men. Revelation shall come. It will come in one area. Then it will come in another and another.

For I am raising up on the earth *specialists in the areas of ministry*. One will minister in the area of love. One in the area of faith. One will minister in another area.

Many will be anointed and brought forth in these days whom I have anointed to deal specifically with certain subjects in My Word. They shall bring forth the revelation of My Word. Some shall deal with forgiveness. Some will deal specifically with prayer, and enlightenment will come.

So it shall be shed abroad in the hearts of men, revelation that shall cause them to rise to new heights where they've never been. So shall they operate in the principles of My Word.

For My anointing shall flow within them. And you shall see the Church, a glorious Church, that shall arise in the midst of chaos, in the midst of turmoil and strife.

In the midst of it will come unity of My Spirit. So shall it flow. For I will make a short work of righteousness on the earth. Then My people shall leave this earth with a blaze of glory, saith the Lord.

Commentary

I am reminded of the gifts of the Spirit and how God decides which person He uses to manifest any of the nine gifts that are listed in First Corinthians 12.

> *All these are the work of one and the same Spirit, who apportions them to each one as He determines.*
> 1 Corinthians 12:11

If there are nine gifts of the Spirit—which are distributed in separate and distinct manifestations—is it any stretch to think that the fivefold ministry gifts would also have separate and distinct functions in the body of Christ? And that it may be further divided into specific subjects?

I can remember hearing conversations over the years between members of the body of Christ. "Why does Kenneth Hagin always preach on faith?" "Why does Charles Capps always have to teach on confession?" "Why does Kenneth Copeland always bring up financial prosperity?"

In the latter days of my dad's ministry when the Holy Spirit gave him an assignment to teach on the end times, it became, "Why does he always teach on prophecy?"

Perhaps people never considered that God gave these and others an assignment and called them to bring that particular message to the body of Christ. If you needed brain surgery, would you go to a foot surgeon? Of course not! But some people need surgery on their feet. And just because that is not what *you need* at the moment does not negate the validity of foot surgeons.

We need *all* the ministry gifts. And we need them functioning in the specific area God has called them and delivering the message He gave them for the Church.

As a believer, you have the right and responsibility to search the Bible for truth and judge every message according to scripture. Ask the Holy Spirit to enlighten and lead you to the truth. He knows what is needed to mature the body of Christ.

Have you ever rejected or spoken dismissively of a certain minister or ministry gift? Even though you may not need or appreciate the message, it is wise to hold your tongue.

> *For he that will love life, and see good days, let him refrain his tongue from evil, and his lips that they speak no guile.*
>
> 1 Peter 3:10 KJV

THE WORLD'S SYSTEM HAS FAILED MY SYSTEM WILL PREVAIL

September 1982

San Jose, California

*"Confusion has come to the world,
for the world has walked in their own way."*

My Word is not void of power, but My people are void of speech. They speak the words of the enemy, and it causes fear to come. Begin to speak My Word. Give My Word voice, and your fears will flee, and My power will abide in you.

My words will cause you to grow in wisdom, in knowledge, and in My grace. My grace is sufficient. My willingness to use My power on your behalf is the same as it was 2,000 years ago. I have not changed.

Speak what I have spoken to you. By doing so, you will tap into the resources that have been given. For I would not withhold any of these things from you.

The enemy would cause you to stumble and fall and not enter into these things at all. But My Word will cause you to prevail.

You will rise above where the world has failed. You will walk in victory. You will walk in life with a new understanding and wisdom when others are confused and in despair.

My wisdom is in My Word. As you walk in the light of it, quote it and speak it. It will come within you and become part of you.

Receive what I have given. Walk in the light of what I have revealed, and more light will come. Your pathway will grow lighter, and your wisdom shall grow more profound.

But those who walk in darkness shall stumble and know not at what they fall. They will rise and stumble again because they walk in darkness.

But as you walk in the light, more light will come. For My light is the true light, so walk in it, and ye will know the truth. The knowledge of this truth will make you free.

Confusion has come to the world, for the world has walked in its own way. The world has come to a place where they know not where to turn.

But if you will gird up your loins in this day and walk in the light of what I have told you to say, keep your words and your heart before Me right. Then you will begin to see what I have promised in days of old.

In the days to come, mighty things will happen, but people will not believe the reports. For you see, the world has walked in their own ways, but My people shall walk in a new way—in My way.

Oh yes, My Word says that "My ways are higher than your ways. Higher than the heavens are above the earth." I am teaching you My ways.

So walk in the light of what is revealed. These things are not new. They were there from the beginning of time. But now, I am putting greater emphasis on these things, for it is time for the light to shine.

Greater light is coming, for I am revealing greater truths and a deeper understanding of My Word. It's the same Word it has been all these years. Some have received it, but some have scoffed at it. Some have laughed at it and trodden it underfoot and gone their own way.

The world system has failed. Don't be disturbed because My system will prevail. So just come up a step higher and walk with Me. Walk on the higher plain.

What the world has done over and over, year after year, they've done it the same. But the things that worked in days past won't work in the end time.

The ways are changing, and the days are changing. My people must walk with Me on a higher plane. For I am leading you to an understanding of the Word far beyond what men have understood in the past.

So gird up your loins. Be faithful to speak what I say regardless of what your mind says, your religious training, and all that people would say. Walk with Me. For as you walk with Me, we together will win.

Commentary

Confusion and despair come from darkness, but we can rise above and walk in the light. As you read these prophecies, you will begin to see a thread that runs through all of them. It's time for us to walk in the light to live in victory.

The more you actually *walk* in the light and speak light, the more light will be given. What you focus on is where you will go and what you will become. God wants His people to walk in victory.

> *But if we walk in the light, as he is in the light, we have fellowship one with another, and the blood of Jesus Christ his Son cleanseth us from all sin.*
>
> 1 John 1:7 KJV

Do you choose to lend your voice to the Spirit by speaking *light* into the darkness in this world?

INVENTIONS OF COMMUNICATIONS IN 1978 USED IN THE MILLENNIUM
FINANCIAL INVERSION IN THE WORLD'S MONETARY SYSTEM BY A SPIRITUAL EQUATION

1978

"Some things that are coming forth in the year 1978 will be things that will be used in the millennium. There are coming forth inventions that men have not understood before."

A financial inversion in the world's monetary system by a spiritual equation operated from the spirits of men walking the ways of My Word, and My authority shall bring forth a fulfillment of prophecy from My Word.

As spiritual equations are understood and put in practice, men will believe for the hundredfold return.

When men begin using the Word of God not just as a sounding board to hear something but in the Spirit, they will set it forth in the areas of their finances, in the areas of their physical body, in the area of the needs of others.

Then the spiritual equation shall come forth, and it shall be in the authority of My Word. It will be beyond the ability of matter to stand against the principles of the Spirit of God in the realm of the world of the Spirit. And it shall be as though it were an explosion in the realm of the Spirit.

As it was in the days when the atom was split and a release of tremendous power was brought forth into this path in your generation, a tremendous force of power that changed the course of this earth and the men's lives that live upon it.

So is there now even so being wrought in the world of the spirit—the splitting of the atom in the spirit world that shall release tremendous power beyond the ability of a man to conceive and beyond the ability of a man to operate in with his intellect.

But they will not operate in the intellect. It will be to those who operate in the realm of the spirit. Those who will set themselves away from the ways of the world and hear the voice of the Spirit of God.

Tremendous truths are coming forth. As man has grasped the knowledge of the physical in the realm of this earth, the inner man—the likeness of God Himself—shall grasp the truths of the eternal God from the world of the spirit.

He shall walk in the realm of understanding that no man has walked in since the beginning of the creation, except one man, the last Adam. These men shall walk in that realm beyond a degree of which any man has fathomed.

The world shall stand in awe, and men shall walk beyond the capabilities of all that has been conceived. Then you will know that the end time is here.

My Word has gone throughout the earth, and there shall be a revelation of My Word throughout this land. Partly because men have tapped the ability to conceive and bring forth what men have said is impossible. They will say it defies the very laws of nature and the laws of relativity.

It will not be so that it defies laws, but in the world of the spirit, it will come. It will be an understanding beyond the capabilities of the human mind.

So far beyond in the realm of communication shall it be that men will be able in one hour to send forth and minister to more men than have been ministered to in the ages before with all the missionaries in the times before.

For it will be so beyond the airwaves and the television and beyond the capabilities of the mind shall it be.

For these are the days of My manifestation. I will give you a glimpse into the world to come. Because it will be so that many of the things that will come out of this as My Spirit moves will be used in the days of the millennium.

WISDOM OF THE AGES AND SECRETS FROM THE FOUNDATION OF THE WORLD

1978

Men's words from the beginning of the fall have been perverted and so the failure has been that men have walked in their own ways. This is the day when the Lord hath revealed the wisdom of God to the hearts of men that have sought Him for true understanding and the desire to walk in the ways of God.

Many have said that God's ways are higher than our ways. They are higher than the heavens are above the earth. It is so. My ways are different and higher than your ways, but I am raising up an army of people who will learn to walk in My ways.

As you learn to walk in the ways of God so shall My wisdom be released within you. So shall it be in the closing days—men shall walk in the paths which no man has walked. And the power of God shall be released in the hearts of men through the faith and the working of My Word.

The laws of My Spirit shall move in the midst of men who will rise to an understanding of the secrets that have been kept from the foundation of the world. So shall they be able to diagram them and bring forth to the hearts of men and before visions of their eyes, upon blackboards, as it were, that they shall reveal the truths of My Word.

Men shall rise to an understanding to a degree of the wisdom of God that I have set apart for the last hour. The day is at hand, for the vision is before My people now. Even now, some are seeing in their spirits things they have not been able to put into words.

But for My people who will walk in the ways of God and give themselves to the purpose of My Gospel, I shall release an understanding that men have not had heretofore.

For it shall be that the ways of men shall fail in this hour as never before. For all that can be shaken will be shaken in these days.

But I say unto you that My Word cannot be shaken. My Word is the way. The ways of God are in My Word, and My ways are your ways, and your ways shall be My ways.

For you will walk with Me, and My wisdom we shall agree. So shall it be in the hours ahead that there shall be darkness, and there shall be trouble and turmoil.

But men shall learn to purpose in their hearts to walk in My ways. It will be as though they were walking a straight line. Neither shall they deviate to the right nor to the left. But they shall walk on even when circumstances look as though they are impossible. They will proclaim and decree it shall be. It shall be, and so shall it be, saith the Lord. For I have risen in the midst of My people.

No, don't say we've heard it before and haven't seen it yet. You have heard it before, and you are hearing it now. Look around you; it is already beginning to come to pass.

For I tell you that men led by the Spirit of God shall be released in an area of understanding of the wisdom of the ages. It shall come forth in this hour. Even now, it's coming to pass in parts of the world.

Some things coming forth in the year 1978 will be things that will be used in the millennium. There are coming forth inventions that men have not understood before.

Even those that shall bring them forth will not understand them. There will be some people who will say it won't work, it won't work.

The educated, the well-learned, and engineers who are trained in their field will wring their hands in despair. They'll not know where to turn. They will look here and there, but the answer is not there. They will say it won't work, but it will work because I have revealed it to My people who will bring it forth.

So lift up your head and rejoice, for you are living in a day that you shall see the things that the prophets of old have said, and some will not believe the reports that will come forth.

For My people shall rise, and the world will stand in awe, for I shall come with great wisdom in power in the midst of My Word.

No, it's not in the ways of the world; it's not in the ways of men. Rejoice and lift up your eyes, for it is in the Word. Let My

Word be the apple of your eye. So shall you see My power in these days, saith the Lord.

Commentary

There was such a flow of prophecy in this meeting that I decided to leave the two separate prophecies together since they were done in the same timeframe. Looking back to 1978 from where we are today, this is quite astounding.

We did not have cell phones, personal computers, GPS in our cars, or even on our airplanes. No email, text messaging, or computer video games. Only the Spirit of God knew the world we were headed into.

To reach the world with the Gospel at that time, you were on the radio, wrote books, or went in person. There was no livestreaming of services or YouTube™.

Try putting yourself back to 1978 and realize how remarkable it was what the Spirit was declaring:

> So far beyond in the realm of communication shall things be that men shall be able in one hour to send forth and minister to more men than has been ministered to in the ages before with all the missionaries in the times before. For it will be so beyond that the air waves and the television and beyond the capabilities of the mind shall it be.

A Glimpse Into the World to Come

> I will give you a glimpse into the world to come. Because it will be so that many of the things that will

come out of this as My Spirit moves will be used in the days of the millennium.

These are some of the things that popped up on an internet search for 1978 inventions:

- Four GPS (Global Positioning System) satellites were launched into space.[1]
- Illinois Bell Company began testing a cellular mobile phone system—advanced mobile phone service (AMPS) in the Chicago area.[2]
- An electronic mail system was created at University of Medicine and Dentistry of New Jersey in Newark, New Jersey.[3]

By the end of the 1970s, a computer scientist began to solve the problem for packet switched computer networks to communicate with one another and integrate into a single worldwide "Internet." He called his invention "Transmission Control Protocol" or TCP. We now know this as the handshake that allows computers to connect (TCP/IP) in virtual space.[4]

NOTES

1. "A Brief History of GPS," aerospace.org, February 2, 2021, https://aerospace.org/article/brief-history-gps.

2. "Illinois Bell Telephone Company," encyclopedia.com, accessed October 22, 2021, https://www.encyclopedia .com/books/politics-and-business-magazines/ illinois-bell-telephone-company.

3. Shiva Ayyadurai, "Innovation Anytime, Anyplace, by Anybody®," accessed October 22, 2021, https://www .inventorofemail.com/history_of_email.asp.

4. History.com eds., "The Invention of the Internet," October 28, 2019, https://www.history.com/topics/inventions/ invention-of-the-internet.

CHAPTER 14

REACHING BEYOND THE VEIL

Wˢe live in a day when we must open our spiritual ears and discern what God is saying. We cannot be complacent. The prophecies I just shared with you contain some amazing statements. But like someone once said, they won't fall on us like ripe cherries off a tree! God requires something of us and that is the action of faith. We must reach out with the hand of faith and take hold of what God has promised. Much is to be learned from Hebrews 11.

Enoch walked in *habitual fellowship with God.* He was not spiritually shortsighted to only see the day that he lived in. Enoch looked across thousands of years—from where he was in Genesis 5 to First Thessalonians 4, where Paul tells us that we will rise to meet the Lord in the air.

Enoch said, "I believe I'll take that right now." He

> **God requires something of us and that is the action of faith.**

partook in an event scheduled thousands of years in the future and was caught up in the air to be with the Lord. How? By faith. In the realm of the spirit, our concept of time does not exist.

Triumphs of Faith

Hebrews 11, that great hall of fame, details how distinguished women and men of faith reached out beyond their time into a future age and laid hold of the fruit of it.

Women received their dead resurrected back to life again when rising from the dead had not yet been made possible by Jesus' resurrection from the dead (see Heb. 11:35).

Sarah received healing and a creative miracle in her body to bear a child in her old age before Jesus had borne our sicknesses and infirmities. She reached from one realm to another, from one dispensation to another by her faith. She pulled into her present time a miracle directed by the Spirit of God and the power of God (see Heb. 11:11).

Abraham looked at the resurrection as a possibility when he acted in faith as he prepared to offer Isaac his son (see Heb. 11:19).

Under God's direction, Moses carried out the sprinkling of the blood of the lamb on the doorposts of the children of Israel before the Lamb (Jesus) had ever been slain (see Heb. 11:28).

They operated outside the natural realm of time and space by reaching into the spirit realm by faith. God is not bound or limited by time, and when we enter God's realm of the spiritual kingdom, neither are we!

Reaching Beyond Time

Scripture tells us that after the Tribulation, we will step into the Millennium. The tree of life whose leaves are for the healing of the nations is there.

> *Then the angel showed me a river of the water of life, as clear as crystal, flowing from the throne of God and of the Lamb down the middle of the main street of the city. On either side of the river stood a tree of life, bearing twelve kinds of fruit and yielding a fresh crop for each month. And the leaves of the tree are for the healing of the nations.*
>
> **Revelation 22:1-2**

We don't have to look at that time and think how wonderful it will be when we get there. Like Enoch, we can reach beyond the veil and pull some aspects of the Millennial dispensation into our realm.

We can say, "I believe I'll take *divine health* right now. No more battling this sickness and that disease. Today, I will access what exists in the world to come and live in constant, divine health."

Inventions and things of the Spirit lie just beyond

God is not bound or limited by time, and when we enter God's realm of the spiritual kingdom, neither are we!

the veil of separation. But we can reach out by faith and bring them into existence now. We are in one realm, and they lie just over in another realm. If we can see it, we can have it. All we have to do is reach out in faith and grab hold of it.

It wouldn't be possible to take something from another dispensation, except it's by faith. It shouldn't have been possible for Enoch to be translated. But it became possible through his faith.

A few years ago, I began to have dreams about inventions, and that I was involved in working on mathematical equations and writing in a foreign language. I was participating in the development stage. I had many dreams about this over the years.

Recently, as I was praying in the spirit and received the interpretation, I realized I was still praying about this invention that was to come forth. I believe that the Holy Spirit will pray through us as we give ourselves to prayer to bring inventions forward that will benefit mankind. I don't believe I am the inventor, but I am reaching for this to come forth in prayer (and evidently in my dreams).

> We can reach beyond the veil and pull some aspects of the Millennial dispensation into our realm.

As I was reading over the prophecies from the 1970s and 1980s, I realized that we shouted about what was said, but did we pray about them? Did we allow the Holy Spirit to pray through us in a heavenly language to bring the prophetic words to pass? It's not too late.

CHAPTER 15

RIVER OF PROPHECY

The spirit of prophecy is like a flowing river. Peter tells us the prophets of old were moved along by the Holy Spirit to speak and declare what was to come.

> *For the prophecy came not in old time by the will of man: but holy men of God spake as they were moved by the Holy Ghost.*
>
> **2 Peter 1:21 KJV**

The flow of the Spirit through prophecy called the future into existence through the seed of the words that were spoken. Every word God speaks will reach its destination and be fulfilled.

Some of my fondest early memories are of the many times my dad took me fishing at the White River in southeast Arkansas. I was always awed by the flow of the streams and rivers that made up the confluence of the Mississippi River.

We would launch the small, flat-bottomed boat from the muddy shore into the swift flow. And when we reached the designated spot, Dad would grab an overhanging limb and tie a rope to it. The force of the water would whip the boat stern around as we prepared to drop our heavily weighted and baited lines into the murky bottom where the catfish were.

While waiting for that familiar tug on the fishing line, I would watch the water current create eddies around fallen trees and eroded areas of the shoreline. Sometimes tree limbs and small branches would float by swiftly going downstream.

> The flow of the Spirit through prophecy called the future into existence through the seed of the words that were spoken.

Once in a while, a piece of driftwood would have its journey interrupted by being caught in one of those eddies. Swirling around and around, it seemed to be forever stuck and unable to break free of the unending whirlpool of water.

It wasn't going anywhere except in circles, but eventually something would happen. Some outside force—like more rain, a sudden flood, or a tree falling—would loose the driftwood from its holding pattern and free it to make its way down the White River to the mighty Mississippi.

If the catfish weren't biting, Dad and I would drag the boat through the wilderness to one of the many oxbow lakes in the White River National Wildlife Refuge. These little lakes had been created when the river changed its course, leaving a curved "oxbow" shape body of water where the river used to flow.

A Spiritual Flow

The river of the Spirit is constantly moving, sometimes overflowing its banks and creating new paths that are unexpected and unanticipated, leaving behind stagnant bodies of water where the fresh current of the river once flowed. Some churches and denominations that once experienced a mighty move of God find themselves still in the water but not going anywhere because they became complacent and liked where they were.

To be in the flow of the River of the Spirit can be confusing at times to the natural mind. As you move along, there are twists and turns you don't expect, and sometimes you feel as though you are caught in an eddy going in circles and making no progress. But the river is still moving, and these obstacles are only temporary diversions.

Many Streams, One Destination

As amazed as I was with watching the current, one day when the fish weren't biting, Dad started the motor, and we went miles downstream to the main river. I was shocked to see that the tributary we had been fishing in was only one of many streams that merged into a great wide flowing river, unlike anything I had ever seen or imagined!

As each individual river or stream merged, it created a massive roiling and tremendous force that moved aside every obstacle on its way to the ocean. Nothing could stop it from reaching its final destination.

Over the years, each outpouring of the Spirit has created a river, and each river flows to a final destination. My great grandparents were a part of the Pentecostal Movement, and my grandparents were part of the Healing Movement. My immediate family became a part of the Word of Faith Movement, which includes all the rivers created by these outpourings.

> **Some churches and denominations that once experienced a mighty move of God find themselves still in the water but not going anywhere.**

Other rivers are moving toward our final destination too. We have been unaware of them and cannot see them because we are in a different stream. We are separated, but we are going in the same direction. There can be no doubt, the ecclesia of the Lord Jesus Christ will reach their destination!

The river of prophecy is also like those rivers. Seeds and words of prophecy are spoken and have yet to be fulfilled. It may appear that they will never be fulfilled and are caught in an eddy for the time being.

We only see what is in our river, and we may not fully understand what is or is not happening. Only through faith do we obtain these promises, knowing that no word of God will return void.

No obstacle can withstand or stop the fulfillment of what God has declared. *The latter rain is falling. Are you ready to flow in His Spirit?*

> *In the last days, God says, I will pour out My Spirit on all people. Your sons and daughters will prophesy, your young men will see visions, your old men will dream dreams. Even on My menservants and maidservants I will pour out My Spirit in those days, and they will prophesy.*
>
> **Acts 2:17-18**

> *So shall my word be that goeth forth out of my mouth: it shall not return unto me void, but it shall accomplish that which I please, and it shall prosper in the thing whereto I sent it.*
>
> **Isaiah 55:11 KJV**

ABOUT ANNETTE CAPPS

Annette **Capps** is the host of the *Concepts of Faith* television program and author of six books, including *Reverse the Curse, Angels,* and the best seller, *Quantum Faith.* As president of Capps Ministries, she continues to expand the ministry founded by her father, author and teacher Charles Capps.

For a complete list of CDs, DVDs, and books by Capps Ministries, write:

Capps Ministries
P.O. Box 10, Broken Arrow, Oklahoma 74013

Toll Free Order Line (24 hours)
1-877-396-9400

www.cappsministries.com

Visit us online for:

Radio Broadcasts in Your Area

Concepts of Faith Television Broadcast listings:
Local Stations, **Daystar**, **VICTORY** & **TCT**
Television Network

E-Books & MP3s Available

youtube.com/CappsMinistries

facebook.com/CharlesCappsMinistries

BOOKS BY ANNETTE CAPPS

Quantum Faith®
(Also available in Spanish)
Reverse the Curse in Your Body and Emotions
Removing the Roadblocks to Health and Healing
Overcoming Persecution

BOOKS BY CHARLES CAPPS
AND ANNETTE CAPPS

Angels

God's Creative Power® for Finances
(Also available in Spanish)

God's Creative Power® – Gift Edition
(Also available in Spanish)

BOOKS BY CHARLES CAPPS

Calling Things That Are Not

Triumph Over the Enemy

When Jesus Prays Through You

The Tongue – A Creative Force

Releasing the Ability of God Through Prayer

End Time Events

Authority in Three Worlds

Changing the Seen and Shaping the Unseen

Faith That Will Not Change

Faith and Confession

God's Creative Power® Will Work for You
(Also available in Spanish)

God's Creative Power® for Healing
(Also available in Spanish)

Success Motivation Through the Word

God's Image of You

Seedtime and Harvest
(Also available in Spanish)

The Thermostat of Hope
(Also available in Spanish)

How You Can Avoid Tragedy

Kicking Over Sacred Cows

The Substance of Things

The Light of Life in the Spirit of Man

Faith That Will Work for You

HOW DOES QUANTUM PHYSICS RELATE TO THE BIBLE?
CAN WORDS MOVE MOUNTAINS?
HOW DID JESUS SUPERSEDE THE LAWS OF PHYSICS?

Quantum Faith by Annette Capps

There are amazing similarities between the teachings of Jesus and the discoveries of the new physics, quantum theory. The concept of speaking to mountains and trees may not be religious metaphor, but laws of a new physics that have not been fully understood.

Jesus taught that our words are powerful enough to move physical matter. Quantum physics has discovered that subatomic particles respond to the observer.

In this book, you will discover that your words and your faith (beliefs) are unseen forces that affect everything in your world. You are the one giving substance to your world through words!

ISBN-13: 978-0-9618975-5-0

Removing the Roadblocks
to Health and Healing

In order to receive healing and live in health, you must prayerfully evaluate your life as a whole and allow the Holy Spirit to guide you into wellness.

In this book, Annette Capps gives a insightful, practical look at the emotional and spiritual hindrances that believers face daily.

Recognizing and removing these road-blocks can enable you to receive healing and walk in health and wholeness.

- claiming sickness as belonging to you
- belief in tribal DNA
- using infirmity as a tool
- holding on to negative emotions
- refusing to forgive
- feeding the spirit of infirmity
- ignoring the leadings of the Holy Spirit and your spirit
- staying in an unhealthy environment
- trying to act beyond your faith
- believing you will be healed in the future

ISBN 13: 978-1-937578-58-9

YOUR CURSE HAS ALREADY
BEEN REVERSED

Reverse the Curse
In Your Body and Emotions

There are many wounded and broken-hearted people in the Body of Christ who are suffering in their mind and emotions. The battleground of Satan's attack has been in the mental arena. Yet there has not been any practical teaching that would guide people into mental and emotional wholeness.

This book will show you how to reverse the emotional curse and in so doing open the door for physical healing and miracles in believers' lives.

Doctors cannot reverse the curse of sickness. Only Jesus can reverse the curse and bring perfect healing and wholeness to an individual's life. Learn how to activate God's power in your body by speaking and acting your faith upon God's Word.

ISBN-13: 978-0-9618975-0-5

The Harrison House Vision

Proclaiming the truth and the power
of the Gospel of Jesus Christ with excellence.
Challenging Christians
to live victoriously,
grow spiritually,
know God intimately.

Connect with us on
 Facebook @ HarrisonHousePublishers
and  Instagram @ HarrisonHousePublishing
so you can stay up to date with news
about our books and our authors.

Visit us at **www.harrisonhouse.com**
for a complete product listing as well as
monthly specials for wholesale distribution.